Accelerate eCommerce Growth

A Proven Framework to Scaling Your eCommerce Business with Digital Advertising

Brendan J. Hughes

Cover Design: Claire Murphy

ISBN: 978-1-9168714-1-0

DEDICATION

Anne, Oisín, Eoghan, Aibhín

CONTENTS

ACKNOWLEDGMENTS

A massive THANK YOU to the range of people who helped with versions of this manuscript. In particular, Katarina White who committed to the concept from the start. Thanks to Claire Murphy for her designs. Thank you also to Cian Fogarty, Max Tomlinson and of course Kevin Stagg who provided great feedback and support. A final thanks to Oisín Hughes who helped with the final proofing to ensure the content was digestible (hopefully he did a good job).

FOREWORD

When I played for and later coached the Ireland rugby team in the early 1990's, we had relatively little data at our disposal to optimize player performance. Today all that has changed. Coaches and backroom teams have access to real-time video analysis, time-lapse software, wearable biometric and GPS tracking, velocity-based training devices, impact sensors and much more. The availability of rich data and instant insights has changed the sport forever.

We've seen the same pattern across every professional sport. The 2011 film, Moneyball starring Brad Pitt, documented just this inflection point for one team in MLB. The movie is based on the 2003 book Moneyball: The Art of Winning an Unfair Game by Michael Lewis, about the Oakland Athletics baseball team and how their fortunes were turned around thanks to innovative use of data in the 2002 season. When competing against the big budgets of others, innovative use of data provides an opportunity to succeed in an otherwise impossible environment. For Oakland, it was a case of how to achieve a lot more with a lot less.

We are now at a point when investment in digital advertising has surpassed investment in traditional advertising channels. When everything is digitized, we might expect greater transparency and control over our investments. However, this is just not the case, thanks in large part to the dominance of a small number of large players who have little incentive to create an open advertising ecosystem. As an eCommerce brand you want to ensure that your target market can easily become aware of your offering and find you when they are ready to purchase. Digital marketers increasingly need to maintain a presence across multiple advertising platforms to reach their target audiences. Ensuring you are getting the best value possible from each platform so you can scale your business efficiently is not easy.

We created Optily to help solve this problem. Optily consolidates and normalizes data from across the ad platforms, putting the advertiser back in the driving seat. The framework outlined by Brendan in this book reflects the learnings from thousands of hours of digital campaign analysis and optimization. The concept of the funnel is familiar to marketers, but Brendan refreshes our understanding of why and how to apply this construct when advertising across today's most relevant digital ad channels. Understanding where to invest time and money to improve performance is a critical task for marketers. The final two chapters of this book narrow in on the key metrics and optimization strategies that we should all keep in mind. I hope you enjoy reading this as much as I have.

- Ciarán FitzGerald, Chairman & Co-Founder, Optily

INTRODUCTION

Bob is a long-time friend who, like many entrepreneurs, is spinning several plates at any one time. He called me a couple of weeks ago to complain about Google. For one of his newer eCommerce projects, Bob had already kicked off some digital advertising. In fact, he had spent around $2,000 per month over eight months on Google Ads without much traction and finally called a halt to it.

Within a few days of pausing the campaign, Bob received the inevitable call from the Google outbound marketing team to understand why he had stopped advertising. During the call, the helpful Googler pointed out that about 80% of his keywords "were never going to do anything for [him]" and this was the source of the problem.

So, of the $16,000 Bob had spent on ads over an eight-month period, he would have had more satisfaction going all in with a pair of deuces at the poker tables he enjoys so much. And he might have had a better chance of a successful outcome too!

Needless to say, Bob decided he's "never giving Google one cent of [his] money in future." Which is a pity. Google is a really great way for any eCommerce company to scale their business.

Now, this isn't a story just about Google. Bob's experience could have been about *any* of the big ad platforms we all rely on to help us accelerate our growth. So why do we hear so many horror stories of businesses being burned by their experiences on these platforms?

The Way it Was and the Way It Is Now

In the days before digital, it was not terribly easy for small businesses to "do" advertising. For a TV, radio ad, or print you needed to speak with someone to arrange and book the placement. Typically, that person had some incentive to advise and ensure you were aligning your spend with your business goals. With the advent of digital, advertising to the world has now become incredibly easy for everyone.

With self-service advertising, we no longer need an intermediary to book and pay for our ads. This is remarkable and presents endless opportunities for small and medium businesses to compete on a global scale. However, no matter how simple the platforms make it for us to purchase ads, the odds remain stacked against the uninitiated.

The incentives across the industry are not aligned well with a small or medium-sized advertiser's goals. The ad platforms, media agencies, and tech intermediaries have all established their business models anchored around the amount that advertisers spend buying ads. Think about it, has any party you've engaged with regarding digital advertising ever advised you to spend less?

In the battle between David and Goliath, the small advertiser is David, and the entire ad industry is Goliath. Goliath has all the assets, all the data and power to maximize the returns from smaller advertisers. It's no wonder that every ad platform makes it incredibly easy for novice advertisers to use their services.

Who will benefit from this book?

Harrison is another pal who is the CFO in a successful consumer business. Harrison is convinced that the ad industry is built upon the inherent principle of waste. The cleverest thing the industry ever did, he suggests, is popularizing the idea that only 50% of advertising doesn't work. In his view the percentage is a lot higher; he suggests closer to 100%.

He's taken this position because he's seen so many dollars spent on advertising with little attributable return. I debate this with Harrison regularly, citing many examples that disprove his conclusion. Personally, I think Harrison takes an extreme view in order to make his point. His real purpose is to elicit from the marketing function a comprehensive justification of advertising spend and reassurance that the investment in advertising is both efficient and effective. We all want that.

This book isn't intended for CFOs and accountants, but for

all those who answer to people like Harrison and are accountable for making efficient and effective digital advertising investments.

You're up and running with your Shopify, Big Commerce, WooCommerce, or Magento store and have had some initial sales traction. Organic sales and maybe even some initial paid media activities are yielding results. You've started to demonstrate to yourself (and your stakeholders) that there might be something in this eCommerce initiative you've started or inherited.

Perhaps you've plateaued or maybe you're ready to make the next step to invest in multiple ad channels in order to grow your business faster. As you reach this point, you want to ensure that you make smart investments both in terms of time and money.

You need a strategy and a plan. The intention of this book is to offer you a framework that helps you compile a digital ad strategy that aligns with your overall business strategy. I'll outline tactics that can help you deliver on that strategy. I'll provide you with the questions and potential answers to those questions that you can use to keep your team on track.

It was the conversation with Bob that prompted me to finally put these pages together. My hope is that Bob, and others like him, find practical insights and data points here which help them to efficiently grow their business with the help of paid digital advertising.

In answer to the persistent challenges from my friend Harrison, I call out the industry where I see willful attempts to disguise waste and, hopefully, set out an approach that is structured around driving maximum efficiency with the highest effectiveness.

Let's tip the balance back in the small advertiser's favor by identifying strategies that help us to reduce the waste and be more efficient with each dollar and hour we spend.

What will you get out of this book?

If you've picked up this book, then you're looking for a practical approach to digital advertising to support your eCommerce business. Read on to access a step-by-step guide to achieving success from the outset.

The vast topic is broken down into seven sections. Each section can be taken in isolation as a reference, but there is a logical sequence here, so I recommend you read through from start to finish. Use the checklist at the end of each chapter as a practical support to ensure you've at least considered all of the activities that will help you deliver success.

In chapter ***#1 Laying the Groundwork***, we'll take a step back and map out the five key pillars we've identified over many years of building and delivering successful digital advertising strategies that are critical to have in place before you get started.

In chapter ***#2 The Funnel is Dead. Long Live the Funnel.***, we map out how a better understanding of consumers' attitudes and behaviors through their digital purchase journey leads to more effective advertising. We demonstrate how a structured approach to your advertising is critical for both more effective and more efficient investments in digital media.

Chapter ***#3 Inspiring Cold Audiences*** identifies how at the upper end of the eCommerce funnel we set out to inspire people about how our unique offering transforms people's lives. The hero is the consumer and a vision of what the future looks like thanks to our product. Digital advertising amplifies our story.

Moving through to chapter ***#4 Educating Warm Audiences***, we see that as consumers research and compare offerings across a category, the digital advertising task is to educate about the differentiating features and benefits of our products. Our advertising nudges in-market shoppers to deeper engagement.

In chapter ***#5 Convincing Hot Audiences***, we emphasize that for shoppers who have demonstrated strong purchase intent, our advertising shifts to overcoming purchase objections, providing clear reasons for purchase now, and personalizing sales messages to the right audience at the right time.

In a multi-channel advertising world, digital marketers continue to struggle with clearly identifying where to invest ad spend right now, to deliver the best returns. In chapter ***#6 Measurement & Attribution***, we map out the options and some straightforward approaches to attributing the contribution of digital advertising to sales.

Finally, in chapter ***#7 Optimization for Growth***, we see that while the ad platforms provide optimization capabilities, very often they don't provide the levels of control that many of us require. We look at effective approaches to manual, automated and cross-channel optimization for growth when advertising across multiple ad channels.

#1

LAYING THE GROUNDWORK

Before we begin, let's chat briefly about the role of paid advertising in your overall marketing mix. Carley is a typical eCommerce entrepreneur who I've gotten to know recently. She has spent around 6 months already in beta mode with her new platform for young moms and has reached out to her own network and influencers to gain some initial traction.

The small amounts of money she has spent on digital ads so far haven't delivered much, which makes her a little nervous about investing more. Growth has stalled and Carley is feeling a little stuck. She feels like the next step is to raise a lot of money in order to go all in with digital ads and scale up. This is risky, as it could be potentially fatal.

Digital advertising is not the first solution to the problem of being stuck. Without a bunch of other foundational elements in place within your eCommerce business, there's a strong likelihood that advertising won't deliver what you expect.

We're not talking about the operational fundamentals of supply chain, customer support, and fulfillment here. So, let's assume the business model is sound. Paid media's role is to **complement an effective owned and operated overall digital marketing strategy**.

The elements if this strategy might include:

- persona development
- customer segmentation
- customer journey mapping
- merchandising
- conversion rate optimization
- content marketing
- search engine optimization
- community engagement
- email marketing
- chat support
- social proof points
- payment and delivery flexibility
- web analytics

This isn't a book about your broader digital marketing strategy, however, before we spend a cent on paid advertising, we like to know certain important building blocks are in place. These building blocks reassure us that if we add fuel to this particular fire, it will truly ignite. If the tinder is damp, because, for example, our product pages are missing some key decision-supporting components, then we will need a lot more fuel to get the fire started and keep it going.

The ad platforms will happily provide that fuel in the form of more eyeballs, but if those eyeballs don't turn into customers at an acceptable rate, then the price we pay for that fuel may be too high for many smaller businesses.

As a managed service solution, the Optily team has been the beneficiary of some early disasters. "My last agency spent a huge amount on digital ads, but I got nothing from it" is not an unfamiliar refrain on early client calls. Agencies aren't all bad and stupid, so the first thing we need do is check that some of those fundamentals are in place before we get started.

Investing heavily in paid media begins to make sense once you've hit your initial growth plateau. You have an eCommerce business model which is starting to work and has the potential to scale if you can only find more customers at an acceptable price.

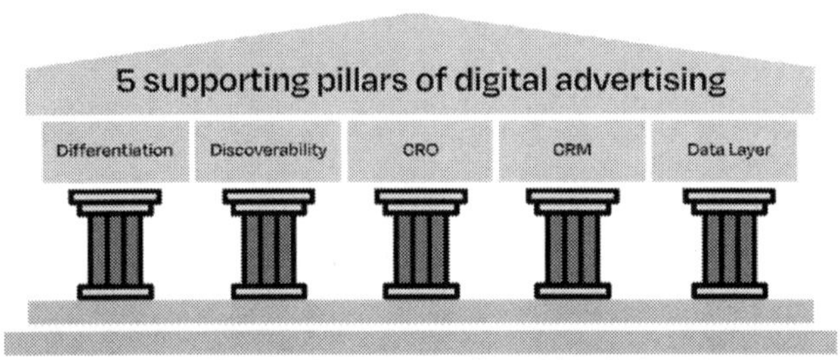

Figure 1 5 supporting pillars of digital advertising

We typically zone in on five supporting pillars of digital marketing. Like any building, once the stabilizing pillars are in place, we find we have a solid business whose growth we can accelerate with paid media.

Pillar 1: Differentiation

Ingvar Kamprad founded IKEA initially to bring locally produced furniture at reasonable prices to his customers. However, when local producers started to boycott his business because he was undercutting them, he was forced to import products from overseas.

Flat-packed delivery became essential to reduce shipping and delivery costs. However, it quickly became the thing that set his business apart. Smaller packaging sizes meant that products could be stocked in the stores where they were displayed and not in warehouses, which now meant that customers could now shop for a wide range of furniture and take them home immediately. This transformed how people furnished their homes.

a. What makes your company stand out?

The very first question we ask any new client about their eCommerce business is: what makes you unique? Everything, I mean **everything**, hangs off the answer to this question. In a nutshell, the more alike you are with other businesses the harder and more expensive every other activity is that comes later.

Distinctiveness is a critical ingredient in marketing effectiveness. As all marketers understand, **short-term efficiencies are short-lived unless fueled by a longer-**

term brand marketing strategy.

Differentiation is not only about highlighting differences in your product, service, or brand. Increasingly for businesses, it is a whole-organization thing.[1] For differentiation to be sustainable, it shouldn't rest in individual offerings or brands, but should be part of how you bring new offerings and brands to market. It's not the output that sets you apart, but the way you do things that brings forth true differentiation. With IKEA you don't just buy another couch or a cabinet, but a means of decision-making, assembly, and delivery.

b. Get Input from Everyone

We know it can often be difficult for an eCommerce company to pull back to having conversations at this level, but clear differentiation really does make everyone's job easier and can save us time and money wasted chasing the wrong customers with the wrong messages. An easy way to start is by getting your team together and aligning on the answers to these six questions:

- **Purpose** - why are we here?
- **Founder story** - where did this start?
- **Solution** - how is our offering different?
- **Pricing** – does our pricing set us apart?
- **Execution** - do we deploy better than others?
- **Brand** - what sets our identity apart?

c. Figure Out Who You're Selling To

The next step is to align on the customer profile(s) for whom this matters most. My favorite device for completing this task is to develop a single or multiple archetypal **buyer persona**. A persona is a composite sketch of a key segment of your target audience. We create a profile of an imaginary customer, based on shared attributes of the segment this profile is intended to represent.

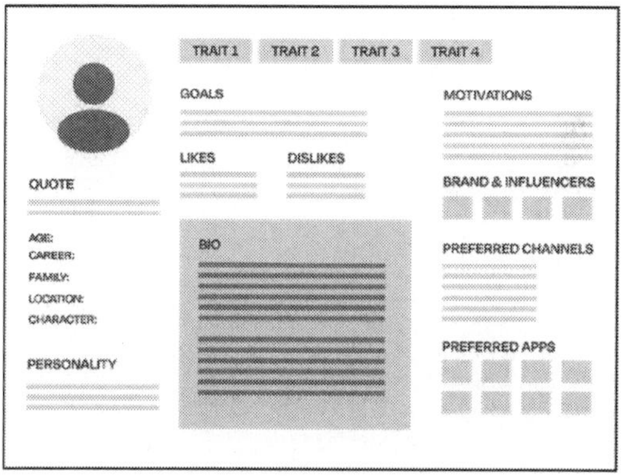

Figure 2 Creating a buyer persona

The creation of a persona[2] is supported by data and research from multiple sources, such as:

- **Primary customer research:** directly engaging with existing or prospective customers and asking them about their purchase attitudes and behaviors.

- **Data analysis:** reviewing historical purchase data, analytics data, or data available from third-party sources, such as our advertising platforms, help us better understand demographics, interests, and behaviors.

- **Customer sales and care teams:** brainstorming with internal teams who are in direct contact with customers daily is a great way to add color to your personas that helps to make them more realistic.

Our buyer persona is not intended to describe an individual customer but paints a picture of our ideal customer. It includes hard descriptors such as demographics, family, and career status. It also includes softer descriptions of their interests and behaviors, relevant to our product.

How do they experience the problem we solve? Where do they find out about solutions? What are their attitudes to pricing and what other types of purchase objections might they have? Developing buyer personas is a critical step that informs much of our later marketing strategy.

d. Align Solutions to Problems

Now clearly articulate how the individual features of your offering deliver benefits for your buyer personas and, more importantly, how these benefits can transform their lives. Put yourself in the shoes of your ideal customer and complete these phrases...

- **Feature** - "With [feature X]"
- **Benefit** - "I can [do Y]"
- **Impact** - "Which enables me to [do Z]"

Mapping this approach to the Ikea story, we might read the

following in an internal feather-benefit-impact statement:

"**With** Ikea's self-service warehouse linked to their website, **I can** research my options online and easily pick up the couch in my own car, **which enables me** to take a lot of stress out of replacing that old couch. All done!"

Feature "With this...	Benefit "I can...	Impact "Which enables me to...
Website catalogue	Research new home furnishing options without needing to travel	Be more relaxed in shopping for new furniture
Self-service warehouse	Easily pick up a new piece of furniture	Take the stress out of replacing that old sofa
Click & collect platform	I can see stock online, and then be assured it is waiting for me in store	Reduce time wasted in going to the store when stock is not available

Figure 3 Develop a Feature-Benefit-Impact matrix

Investing time up front in clearly articulating features, benefits, and impacts will be very helpful later as we set out to communicate different messages to consumers, depending on which stage of the purchase journey they are at. For each feature (whether unique or not) of your offering, complete the Feature-Benefit-Impact analysis.

Everything about the IKEA founding story, through to their unique digital offering today, is consistent and enables marketing and advertising teams to create compelling customer experiences. Differentiation helps us better understand the target customer - who they are, where they are, what their pain points are, what appeals to them, and how and when they like to purchase.

Without the clarity of how you are different, your costs to acquire new customers will be unnecessarily high and your activities will be completely focused on lower funnel (and expensive) auction dynamics. We need to be able to create an emotional connection with consumers which can supplement the purely rational decision-making that drives much of Internet shopping behaviors today.

Pillar 2: Discoverability

Do you know many visitors to your website arrive and then leave immediately without viewing more than one page? The industry "bounce rate" benchmark for eCommerce is between 20-45%. Traffic from advertising is nearly twice as likely to bounce as those who arrive from an email you've sent them.[3]

So, potentially up to half of our eCommerce store visitors have one simple interaction and then leave. Coupled with the realistic expectation that between 94-98% of visits to our website will end without a sale, then the necessity to make it easy for people to **find us again** is hopefully obvious.[4]

Let's start with the premise that (almost) **no customer will**

purchase from us on the very first time they click through an ad that they encounter somewhere randomly on the Internet. With this in mind, we can quickly see how important it is for customers to be able to find us again quickly at a later time, on a different device, in a different location.

There are a whole range of things to consider here, but for most the focus is on relative ranking in organic search listings on platforms, such as Google, Bing, and Yahoo!. Yes, we will need to become (or hire) an expert in SEO (Search Engine Optimization).[5]

The more **distinctive and memorable** our first impression is, the easier it will be for potential customers to find us. Start with an identity that is unique and easy to remember, say, and spell. We know this sounds obvious, but we regularly see small and medium sized businesses with identities that are complicated, hard to say or spell and far from unique.

Abhishek operates a local food production company with international ambitions. We met recently at one of the many virtual marketing conferences that are taking place these days. Within the first few seconds of our initial conversation, I found myself on the (wrong) website, belonging to a major US food company with the same name as Abhishek's business. It was time to rethink the name for Abhishek's wonderfully unique offering.

A **unique identity** means that organic search ranking for your own brand name will be much easier. Very often, we see new companies ~~spending~~ wasting money on pay-per-click advertising against their own brand terms on search engines.

It's one thing to defend yourself against competitors advertising against your brand terms, but it makes very little sense to have to spend money on your own name, because you chose one that is too generic or commonly used. The money (and creativity) you may need to spend to acquire a unique domain name, will pay dividends in the short to medium term in reduced ad spend.

Assuming you've nailed it for your own brand terms, **SEO for eCommerce** is focused on maximizing your discoverability and driving traffic from search engines from as many different search terms as possible for your products. It really is a big deal; invest up-front and save money later. Check out my colleague Cian's nice summary on the top "8 things you can do to boost your eCommerce SEO" in the Optily blog, and use this as a guide for conversations with your SEO guru.[6]

Your discoverability is enhanced by claiming as many **social handles** as possible, as soon as possible. In this way, when someone searches for your brand term, not only are they finding your website, but that first page of search results is stuffed full of your footprint.

Simple activities such as establishing a well-structured presence on Google My Business, Bing Places, and Yahoo! Localworks give you instant visibility on key search platforms. In addition, remember that for many users, platforms such as YouTube, Facebook, Instagram, and Pinterest, are the search engines of preference. After Google, YouTube is likely the second most popular search engine on the planet.[7]

Customer review sites and other **business directory listings** will become an ongoing part of your daily eCommerce growth activity. Search engines love user-generated content and, so, it is inevitable that for your brand search terms, these platforms will jump right up there to the top of the first page of search results. Make the most of the platforms that are relevant to your business by creating your profiles there early-on and clearly articulating who you are, how you're different, and with direct links back to your eCommerce store.

Sustaining a long-term **content marketing strategy** is seen by many as critical to enhancing not just discoverability but establishing trust in your brand. 70% of consumers want to find out about your products through content over ads.[8]

Show your customers more interesting content that presents you as an authority in your industry category. Create content that educates about how your products are different. Through your blog, newsletters, social outreach, and product pages, you can reinforce how you are unique and make yourself more findable to boot.

Pillar 3: Conversion Rate Optimization

"Conversion rate" is the percentage of visits / visitors / sessions on our website that result in a sale. We've seen that for eCommerce, we could expect minimum conversion rates anywhere between 2.5 - 4.0%. The economics of conversion rate optimization (CRO) are relatively simple.

If it costs you $15.00 to drive a paying customer to your

website, you can double your sales by spending twice as much on advertising *or* you could double your conversion rate. By doubling your conversion rate, you can spend the same amount of money and deliver twice as many sales. Sweet! The great news about this is that for many websites, improvements to conversion rate don't need to cost a lot of money.

The typical CRO quick wins we look out for with our eCommerce clients include:

- **Design** - in addition to an overall clear and professional design, having very clear calls to action (CTAs) is essential. Very often we see wonderfully designed eCommerce stores, but with little in-page differentiation. We often hear designers complain about how optimization nerds destroy their pages, but if the "Add to Cart" or "Checkout Now" buttons blend in with the rest of the page, it makes everyone's job much harder.

- **Mobile** - at least half of online transactions are now taking place directly on mobile devices.[9] In our offices and stores we tend to live on our laptops and desktops and often not enough attention is paid to mobile user experience. This has been compounded by the (false) belief that people are not willing to convert on mobile devices. There are good reasons why conversion rates on mobile might be lower for you. Number one might be that the mobile experience sucks! Invest in making it easier for customers to search for and browse products. Ensure it is easy for them to add products to cart and complete the checkout process.

- **Speed** - are you concerned about the bounce rate on your site? Well did you know that one of the things you can do to have the greatest impact on bounce rate is ensure your site loads fast? You can reduce your bounce rate from 38% to 9% by reducing page load time from 5 seconds to 2 seconds.[10] That's a fourfold improvement in just 3 seconds! Simply plug in your website URL to Google PageSpeed Insights tool to retrieve some quick hints on what you need to do. If you need convincing that this matters, check out how Amazon's home page on mobile and desktop load in under 2 seconds.[11]

- **Detail** - a former boss of mine, John, who founded a highly successful retail business, always used the mantra "retail is in the detail." What he meant by this was, there is a necessity to obsess about details, when it comes to product merchandising. Photography displaying products from multiple angles, descriptive product videos, seeing the product in context, and precise product specifications have all been shown to have a positive impact on conversion rates.[12]

- **Social Proof -** A whopping 95% of customers read reviews before making a purchase and 72% of customers won't take any buying actions until they've read reviews.[13] Authentic reviews that provide a balanced view of the strengths and weaknesses of your offering are a must before we get started. Customer testimonials, aggregated star ratings, and professional third-party reviews all contribute to improved conversions.

- **Payment, Delivery & Returns -** all eCommerce advertising campaigns are ultimately measured by their capability to drive conversions and revenue. Making sure customers don't fall at the final hurdle because you're not providing enough payment options or are charging too much for shipping. This would result in most expensive advertising being a wasted investment.

- **Exit Overlays** - you've spent a lot of time and money getting shoppers to your eCommerce store and it looks like they're about to leave (and potentially never come back). An exit overlay (or exit-intent overlay) is a screen or pop-up designed to win back a reader's interest before they abandon your website. Done right, they can have a dramatic impact on conversion rates.[14]

- **Automated & Human Chat** - your customers prefer to self-serve, but they'll inevitably have a question that you didn't manage to answer effectively on site. Providing a live text chat box is a brilliantly efficient way to support customers who are getting stuck. However, you can't be online 24/7, so you do need to invest in an automated chatbot solution.[15]

Conversion rate benchmarking will become a central part of your advertising strategy. Optimization of budget spend will focus, among other things, on channels that drive the highest conversion rates.

Analyzing and understanding conversion rates by channel, product, and customer segment will become your daily bread and butter so get started early!

Pillar 4: Customer Relationship Management

Within eCommerce, Customer Relationship Management (CRM) is a term used to encapsulate the range of tactics we deploy to leverage customer data to re-engage them either for an initial or repeat purchase.

At its simplest, CRM involves capturing contact information, which is used, typically through automated tools, to **provide relevant and timely messages** in order to nudge customers towards our conversion goals. So why do we as advertisers look for a meaningful CRM strategy?

Our primary task as advertisers is to acquire new customers, however, as we've already seen, most users don't convert on that first visit to our online stores. We've also seen that the conversion rate from email is among the highest by referral source. Furthermore, returning visitors to an eCommerce website will have nearly twice the Add-to-Cart and

Conversion rates as new visitors to the same site.[16]

So, one quick way to ensure your advertising dollars are not wasted is to ensure that when you ***do*** attract users to your store, you capture contact details as early as possible in the purchase journey and use those details for meaningful and personalized follow-ups.

Collecting contact information

An anonymous user arrives at your web store and you'd really love to gather their contact details before they leave. You know why you want their details, but what's in it for them?

One of the most used tactics for contact list-building within eCommerce is the use of a pop-up on your landing page that offers a one-time discount to new customers on their first purchase. Mick and the team at major automotive retailer, Mick's Garage, are so convinced about this that they've baked their email list-builder, "Want $5.00 off your order?" into their main navigation.

You won't always need to pay, but an eCommerce brand that is willing to pay customers to opt-in to their email newsletter is one who knows the value of being able to communicate directly with potential customers.

Using contact information effectively

Over half of eCommerce brands send a minimum of between 2 and 4 different types of triggered emails with the highest click-to-conversion rate of 21.8% coming from "abandoned cart" emails.[17]

In addition, we see many brands effectively using "product abandonment" and "back in stock" emails. Most impressive results are seen by brands who manage to implement personalization within their triggered emails. Retailers can achieve a whopping 142% increase in revenue per email by using personalized one-time sends.[18]

The average revenue per visit for U.S. eCommerce stores grows from $2.06 to $5.22 for returning visits. The value jumps to a massive $10.54 per visit by customers who have made a previous purchase.[19]

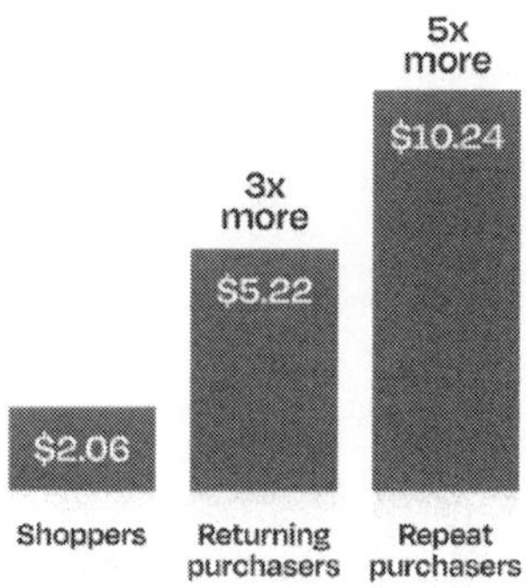

Figure 5 Average revenue per purchase

As we start to consider the true return on investment (ROI) from digital advertising, ensuring your internal processes can maximize customer lifetime value, means you will have more funds at your disposal to acquire those customers in the first place. In short:

- Collect emails and phone numbers as early in the

sales process as possible
- Incentivize the collection of contact details where you know the value they can bring
- Ensure you are collecting adequate consent to use the details as you plan to
- Develop a program to regularly communicate with your contact list
- Personalize contacts based on the recipient's previous actions.

Pillar 5: Data Layer

Your **data layer** is the behind-the-scenes structure that provides access to timely and consistent data flows between your website and other applications. It is a layer as it sits between your website (or app) and the range of other applications that support your website such as analytics, email marketing, advertising, or transactional systems.

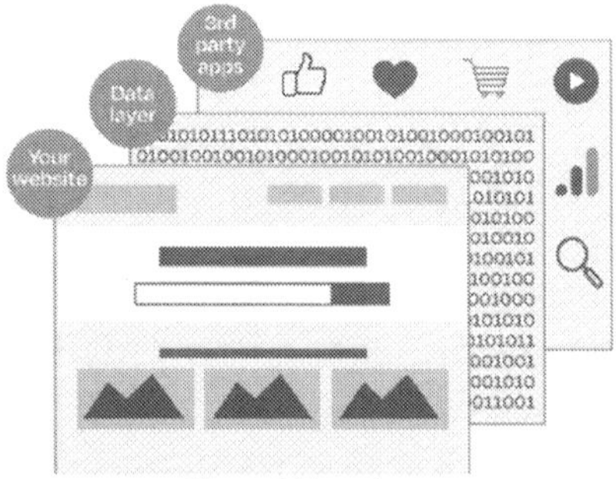

Figure 6 Data layer

The types of data flowing through a data layer can be numerous and varied, consisting of things like eCommerce transaction information, web behavioral data, and mobile application usage. A performant data layer is critical for advertising effectiveness in today's data-driven ad ecosystems.

Unfortunately, it is no longer as simple as implementing ad platforms' tracking pixels or cookies on our website or app. With increased global concern over individual privacy and the resultant regulations such as Europe's General Data Protection Regulation (GDPR) and ePrivacy Directive (ePD) and the California Consumer Privacy Act (CCCP), plus privacy moves from big platforms such as Apple and Google, establishing and maintaining our data layer has never been more complicated.

As advertisers, we want to understand which ads are driving people to purchase via our website or app so that we can sharpen our investment. We want to be able to remarket to people who have demonstrated interest in our offering to encourage them to make that final purchase decision in our favor. To achieve this, we need data flowing in a timely and consistent manner between our website and the various ad platforms we use.

This commercial need must be balanced with an **individual's privacy rights**. In short, we need to inform our website visitors what data we are collecting in our data layer, how that data is being used by us and the ad platforms and confirm their consent for this usage.

While the principles are relatively straight-forward, the implementation approach is changing constantly due to the rapidly evolving privacy regulations and the responses of the various platforms.

Many eCommerce stores today have deployed **tag containers** such as Google Tag Manager (GTM) to help process data from their website's data layer. GTM is one small snippet of code that you insert onto your website which can control how and when other tracking tags are fired on your website.

Think of the GTM tag as a container for all other tracking tags ensuring that all data is collected and processed in a consistent manner. By connecting the GTM container with the tagging interfaces of your various ad and analytics platforms, you can control from a single application how all other applications collect and process user data.

GTM cannot determine which personal data points an individual has consented to being processed by you in this way, so you will need to also implement a **consent management application** on your website.

Consent management platforms such as OneTrust, CookieBot and Quantcast enable you to easily provide full transparency and control to users of your website on how their data is collected and processed. Once your consent management platform of choice has been implemented on your website or app, GTM will only trigger data collection for individuals who have provided the right level of consent.

Much of the privacy debate has revolved around the deployment of third-party cookies on websites. However, it is clear that we need to plan for a world without third-party cookies.[20] Apple's iOS 14 update in 2020, introduced a wide range of new restrictions on user tracking by third-parties such as Facebook and Instagram.

Google's ongoing commitment to eliminating third-party cookies within the Chrome browser is a further indication that the future is cookieless.[21] In response, Google Ads is developing new ways of improving the performance of interest-based advertising that they suggest is at least 95% as effective as cookie-based advertising.[22]

And Facebook is advocating the adoption of their Conversion API which overcomes the issues associated with cookie tracking by connecting your eCommerce server directly with Facebook's servers.[23]

While the ultimate solution is unclear, there is commitment from across the advertising industry to find solutions that both help advertisers deliver effective campaigns, while at the same time respecting individuals' rights to determine how their personal data is collected and used.

- - -

Does this all seem like a lot to ask, before we even get started with digital advertising? Time and again, we see that when brands have at least these five pillars in place, the efficiency of their ad spend is greatly increased.

Being clear and consistent in your uniqueness means less money and time is wasted chasing the wrong customers with the wrong messages. Being easy to find, once a prospective customer has been introduced to your brand saves you immediate ad dollars in helping them navigate back to your site. Improving your capability to convert customers who land on your web store, means you can spend a lot less to achieve more sales.

Initiating personalized trigger-emails to entice users or existing customers to return is a particularly cheap way to improve conversion rates and lifetime value. Deploying a performant data layer that addresses privacy concerns ensures you have the right data available to you to make the right investment decisions.

#1 Checklist

- → Identify how your **business is different** by documenting our unique purpose, founder story, solution, pricing, execution, and brand.
- → Define your key **customer personas** with a mix of customer research, data analysis, and input from custom sales and care teams.
- → Map your product **solutions to problems** by detailing how each product feature, brings a specific benefit and how it impacts peoples' lives.
- → Become **discoverable online** by implementing SEO, claiming social handles, activating review platforms, and through content marketing.
- → Improve your **conversion rate optimization** with clear design, speed optimization, and decision supports, such as chat and social proof.
- → Implement a **customer relationship management** strategy aligning with advertising to nurture customers on their purchase journey.
- → Implement a **privacy-compliant data layer** that enables you to effectively connect customer data across your website and key applications.

#2

LONG LIVE THE FUNNEL

The concept of the "marketing funnel" has been around for over a hundred years. Over that time, it has been variously adapted and attacked. Consumer behaviors in a digital era have changed radically from the 1800's, however the scientific fundamentals that inspired the first iteration of the marketing funnels remain largely unchanged.

We are funnel-believers and will fight to the death all those funnel-killers out there!

The marketing funnel is a construct that suggests customers typically pass through several stages of mental and emotional engagement with a brand or product prior to making a purchase.

The original marketing funnel, proposed by ad agency exec Elias St. Elmo Lewis in Philadelphia back in 1898, suggested four key sequential stages, Attention, Interest, Desire and Action; sometimes shortened to AIDA:[24]

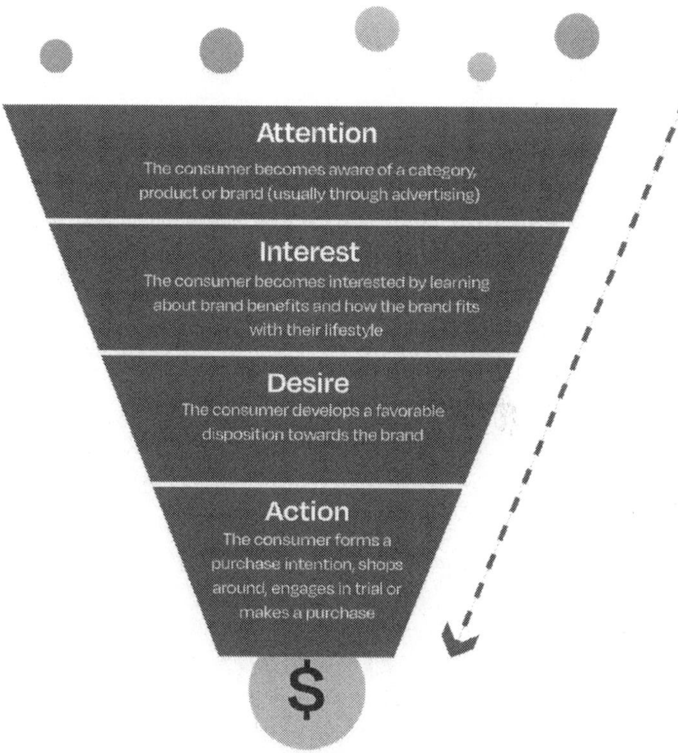

Figure 7 The traditional purchase funnel

The purpose of the funnel for Lewis, in his fledgling ad agency, was to shape how he structured his clients' ad campaigns. For Lewis, the advertiser's purpose was to **attract attention, maintain interest, create desire** and, ultimately, **get action**.

Lewis famously wrote about the challenges of advertising in the early 20th century: "Today we are on the eve of another era of education in advertising. Manufacturers are going out among the great mass of people who refused to be stampeded by the cry of the past hour - and their advertising is going to create desire in the minds of careful folks, and the sales force is going to be organized and educated to cash in on that desire."

The job titles and tools may have changed, but the fundamental interdependence between advertisers and their colleagues in sales (eCommerce) has changed little in over 100 years.

With the advent of the Internet, the funnel concept has been increasingly criticized as being overly simplistic because superficially it suggests that all customers migrate through the exact same steps on their path to purchase. In an increasingly complex age when brand and product messages can appear in so many different and uncontrolled environments, this criticism is particularly profound. It's simply not true that we can map out the exact steps a customer will take on their path to purchase.

A team of Google analysts recently released an insightful report on user journeys having analyzed massive amounts of click-stream data. The summary finding is unsurprisingly that **no two customer journeys are alike**.

However, they did find some surprising results for the sheer volume of "touchpoints" that many shoppers engage with on their path to purchase. One shopper, for example, had 375 touchpoints on their path to purchase personal headphones, while another had 125 touchpoints on their journey to purchase makeup.[25]

On the flip side, many purchases consumers make today are

apparently instantaneous. Nearly half (44%) of American shoppers have made at least one "unintended impulse purchase" in the past three months.[26]

So, while it's clear that the concept of a rigid linear path to purchase is not reflective of how consumers actually purchase today, does that mean the marketer's job reverts back to a spray-and-pray approach?

Many funnel-killers advocate the concept of a "marketing maze" to replace the tried and tested funnel, reflecting the highly unstructured steps consumers may take on their path to purchase.[27] We don't buy into this fully. A structured approach to supporting customers on their purchase journey, using both paid and unpaid media, remains highly valuable.

Regardless of the exact steps taken by a consumer prior to purchasing your product, a marketer's job is to understand consumers' attitudes and behaviors throughout their purchase journey and adapt their strategies accordingly.

Consumer Cognitive & Behavioral States

Researchers and behavioral scientists are broadly aligned on the key cognitive and behavioral stages that consumers pass through prior to purchase.

Understanding these cognitive stages enables us as marketers develop strategies to address the consumer's emotional and rational state.

The modern purchase decision journey can be summarized into these three stages:

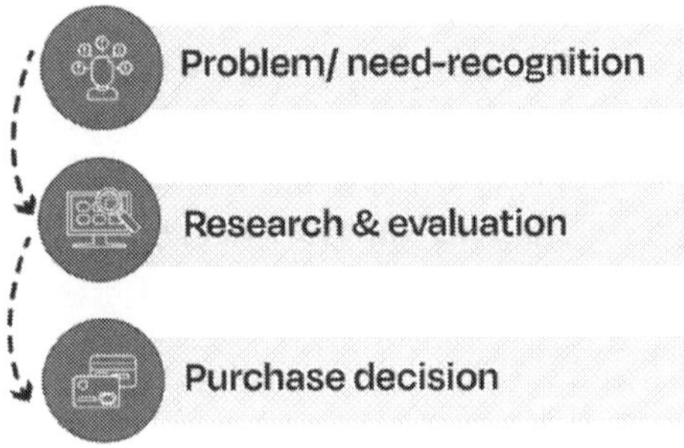

Figure 8 Customer purchase journey

Problem/need/desire recognition – This the first step in the buying decision is for an individual to become aware of the gap between their current state and a preferred state. Without initially identifying that they have a problem to be solved, a need to be fulfilled or a desire to be satisfied, a consumer is unlikely to be enticed to purchase a product.

↓

Research & evaluation – Once a consumer has identified a gap, the next step they undertake is information gathering around the problem and possible solutions. Alternatives will be researched and evaluated against each other. Active evaluation stage begins as people evaluate, add, or subtract goods, products, and services from their consideration sets.

↓

Purchase decision – The third stage is the actual

decision to make the purchase. The consideration set has been narrowed right down and the purchase decision is triggered. Research indicates that one of the most disruptive factors, potentially positive or negative, on a purchase decision is the feedback on a chosen product or brand from peers.

Human decision-making is not linear and at each stage of the purchase journey a myriad of considerations is at play. The final purchase decision is a critical stage. Recent research from The Behavioral Architects demonstrates that cognitive biases play a significant role in the ultimate choice of one product over another.[28]

This research amongst 310,000 real in-market shoppers revealed these six cognitive biases that we need to be aware of as we seek to nudge customers to buy from us:

1. **Category heuristics:** Short descriptions of key product specifications simplify purchase decisions.
2. **Power of now:** The longer you must wait for a product, the weaker the proposition becomes.
3. **Social proof:** Recommendations and reviews from others can be very persuasive.
4. **Scarcity bias:** As stock or availability of a product decreases, the more desirable it becomes.
5. **Authority bias:** Being swayed by an expert or trusted source.
6. **Power of free:** A complementary gift with a purchase, even if unrelated, can be a powerful

motivator.

Some shoppers may pass through the three stages of the purchase journey in an instant and buy in a single session. Others may take weeks and be far more methodical in clarifying their own needs, researching options, and confirming that final purchase decision.

Regardless of the length of time taken or the number of touchpoints engaged with, our advertising is ready to support shoppers through the different emotional and rational steps on the path to purchase.

While eCommerce funnels come in all shapes and sizes, we have learned over many years and thousands of ad campaigns that for maximum ROI, the most effective cross-channel ad campaigns always support the above three phases of consumer purchase behavior.

Supporting the Consumer Journey

Even if we are lucky enough that a consumer undertakes all three phases in a single impulse interaction, our task is to ensure advertising is optimized to support the various psychological needs at each stage.

While we do structure our approach linearly, we are conscious that consumers may step into our world at any point in their personal purchase journey and we are ready for that. For example, where a customer has never seen an ad from us and has jumped straight to the point of purchase without completing the purchase, we want to avoid presenting them with upper funnel messages. We're already past that. Instead, we want to personalize our marketing messages to them based on everything we already know about them based on their on-site activities.

Our three-stage marketing funnel seeks to **inspire, educate and convince** digital consumers to purchase from us:

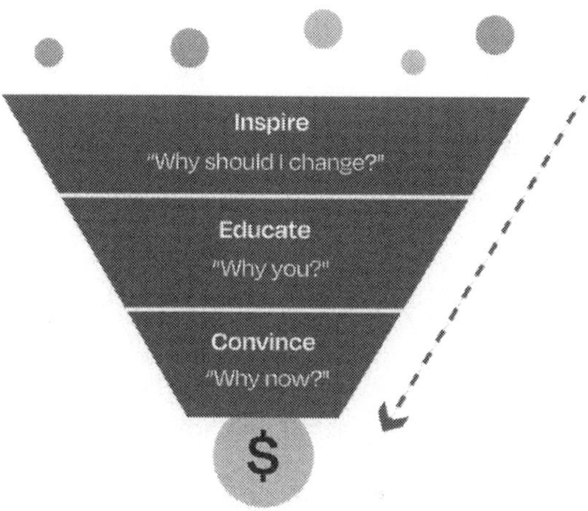

Figure 9 Modern three-stage funnel

Inspire - Upper funnel advertising is concerned with identifying consumers who may be in-market for our solution but are **unaware** of our offering or even that there *are* solutions to the problem they experience. We want to inspire "cold" audiences with the idea of our product making them aware of who we are and what sets us apart.

In communicating at this point of the funnel, we want to address the question in a person's mind of "Why should I change?" Here we focus on how we and our offering are on a mission to transform people's lives. We create a vision for how your life will be impacted by our offering.

↓

Educate - Middle funnel activities address audiences who are aware of our or competitor offerings but are not yet at the point of making a purchase decision. They require **more information** to support their decision-making as they undertake more research and compare us with alternatives. We want to actively educate "warm" consumers as they consider their options about what makes our solution so great.

Our communications here are focused on answering the question of "Why you?". Messages are anchored around specific benefits that can be achieved through our product or service. Our feature-benefit-impact table is a useful tool here for developing messaging pillars.

↓

Convince - Lower funnel tactics seek to address shoppers with **high purchase intent**; helping them overcome purchase objections and nudging them to make that final purchase decision in our favor. Our goal is to convince "hot" audiences to convert on our store right now.

Here, we are addressing the shopper's question of "Why now?" They're somehow bought into your offering but are lacking the urgency to commit. What aspects of our offer are we able to leverage to nudge highly engaged shoppers across the line? Addressing cognitive biases such as authority, urgency, scarcity, and social proof are important here.

Our advertising strategy complements the range of other eCommerce marketing activities that support consumers through these stages.

Customer Journey Maps

Customer Journey Maps are helpful visual tools that enable all team members to align around a customer-centered perspective on the purchase funnel.

Building these journey maps together with all stakeholders ensures maximum understanding and buy-in from marketing, advertising, and eCommerce teams.

A journey map will identify at each stage of the funnel what the customer is:

- **Doing** – what activities are they engaged with? Identifying where they are and what they are doing, enables you to seek to interrupt them in the right place at the right time.

- **Thinking** – what thought process is likely to be taking place? Understanding this enables you to better shape messaging that speaks to their rational mind.

- **Feeling** – what emotions are taking place? Our offering will likely solve some frustration or fulfill some desire for a customer. What are they feeling without that?

Start by identifying a key persona you want to focus on. In practice, you may have different journey maps for each of your most important personas.

Share a blank template with each of your team members individually and encourage everyone to complete it individually at first. Then, together as a team, build out a unified journey map for each persona.

Here's an example of the customer journey map structure we like to use:

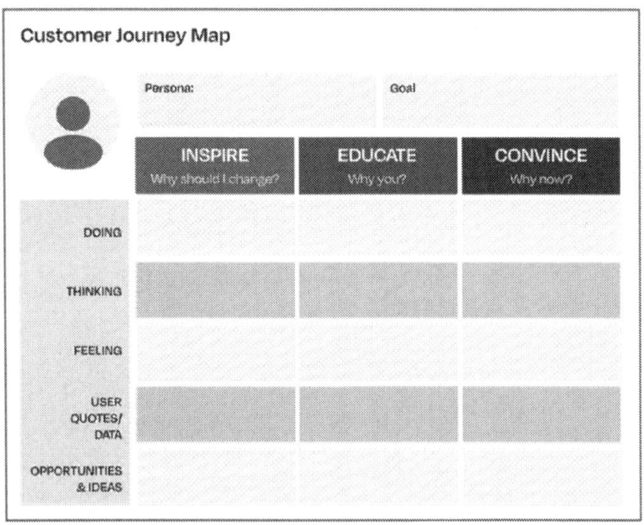

Figure 10 Develop a customer journey map

Funnel Efficiencies

In practice, the most common barrier to the effective use of any funnel structure is the demand to drive lower funnel metrics. Many eCommerce teams will ask why we don't **just focus on lower funnel activity**, since conversion value is the ultimate metric that is being applied to everyone?

In many instances, our businesses are under real pressure to quickly get to significant positive returns from advertising and we know that lower funnel activities deliver the highest returns, since that is what they are designed to do. The simple answer is that we need to feed the funnel.

Consumer engagements at the lower end of the funnel are more expensive and, therefore, we don't want to waste precious ad dollars on conversion activities amongst anonymous users who have shown little or no intent towards our product.

It costs significantly less to leverage creative formats and placements that effectively get our brand in front of broad audiences at the top of the funnel in order to identify those displaying interest in our product.

If we don't put in the effort to inspire and educate audiences around our offering, the lower funnel campaigns quickly run out of steam and become terribly inefficient.

For example, on average, it costs you:

- $0.01 to **inspire** an in-market individual with a 15-second video and inspire them with your offer.
- $0.10 to **educate** an engaged individual enough for

them to click on your ad and visit your website.

- $1.00 to **convince** an individual to make that final decision in your favor and purchase your product.

So, it costs you 100-times more on average to convince someone to purchase (lower funnel goal) than it does to reach previously unknown individuals and engage them in your offer (upper funnel goal). And it costs 10-times more on average to drive engaged audiences to your website (middle funnel goal), than it does to find new people who have an interest in your offer.

That $1.00 to convert a customer is well-spent when you are already addressing the right audience. But you certainly don't want to spend that type of money on people who have no awareness of your product and who have demonstrated no intent to purchase in this category or indeed from you.

Immediately you do try to spend only in the lower funnel, inevitably the $1.00 quickly rises, as you are delivering conversion messages to broad audiences with low intent. Time and again we see that even small investments in upper and lower funnel activities pay huge dividends on lower funnel metrics.

Funnel Investments

So, how much should you invest at the different stages of the funnel? **Marketing Effectiveness** is a hot topic right now, thanks in large part to the work of marketers Les Benet and Peter Field.[29] Benet and Field's research indicates that market share growth is driven by a 60:40 balance between brand-building and sales activation engagements across media channels.

In their arguments for **increased mass-marketing budgets** (upper funnel), their research concludes that firms that cut brand budgets and try to rely on short-term activation consistently underperform in the long term against their peers.

Their message is if you invest only in lower funnel marketing activities you may achieve short-term sales, however, without an effective balance with upper funnel investments, your capability to grow in the longer term is severely hampered.[30]

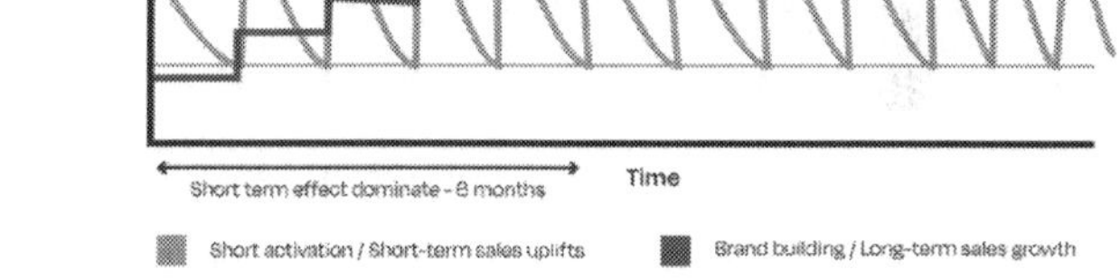

Source: Les Binet and Peter Field, Media in Focus: Marketing Effectiveness in the Digital Era, IPA, (Figure 02)

Figure 11 Marketing effectiveness research findings

In our experience, very few digital native companies are prepared to invest a whopping 60% of digital marketing budgets in longer term brand-building and only 40% in activations, which can be directly measured against short-term sales targets.

One takeaway from this greatly informative research is that it helps internal advertising teams to justify more investment in upper funnel than might otherwise be considered.

An effective funnel strategy finds the right budget balance for each brand, so let's look at the overall framework and how you might apply it to your unique situation.

Remember, **advertising doesn't act in isolation**. The role of advertising throughout the funnel is to support the other owned and operated activities being managed by the broader eCommerce marketing teams.

Within the upper funnel, our understanding of our customers and our ability to stand out from the crowd is essential. Inspiring audiences around our brand with well-crafted human stories based on what makes us different is critical as consumers move through the research and purchase phases.

As consumers research product alternatives, advertising steps in to **keep our brand, key product features, and benefits top of mind**. In parallel, being easily findable and having well-honed website conversion tactics ensure that advertising can take a cost-effective supporting role and not an overly expensive leading role.

At the bottom of the funnel, our ability to identify and communicate with the consumer segments displaying the highest propensity to convert or yield the highest lifetime values is essential to maximizing our marketing contribution.

Marketing Contribution through the Funnel

Marketing Contribution is a financial measure of the profitability of your business after marketing costs have been deducted. Finance buffs will use it as a metric to either beat you up or encourage you to scale up. If your marketing efficiency is good, they might even give you more money to spend on marketing. Imagine!

For most of us non-finance heads, we turn marketing contributions on its head and talk about ROAS (Return on Ad Spend). Whichever metric you are using, the key question is how much of our sales revenue are we in a position to invest in advertising and marketing? What can we afford to spend to acquire a sale?

(In my experience, marketers never seem to have enough money for everything they want to do, so our task is to make the best use of available budgets.)

ROAS is defined as the amount of revenue generated for every dollar spent on advertising and related costs. A ROAS of 10x, means that for each $1.00 spend on advertising, $10.00 in revenue can be attributed back to that advertising.

$$\text{ROAS} = \frac{\text{Revenue from advertising}}{\text{Cost of advertising}}$$

(Return on Ad Spend)

Figure 12 Calculating Return on Ad Spend

Most eCommerce retailers set a minimum expectation of 5x-

10x ROAS across their activities. This means that for every $1.00 in ad spend, they need to be able to account for at least $5.00 or $10.00 in revenue. Somewhere in the business's financial plans, an assumption has been made that we'll need to invest around 10-20% of sales revenue in marketing to acquire new customers.

One thing to keep in mind is that the eCommerce industry is gradually moving away from more simplistic measures such as Cost Per Acquisition (CPA) and Customer Acquisition Costs (CAC). These measures don't consider the revenue value of a new customer, only the cost to acquire an individual customer regardless of how much they are worth.

Focusing on ROAS shifts the analysis to seeking an understanding of which channels are driving the highest value customers either by average order value (AOV) or a total customer lifetime value (CLV).

AOV and CLV are metrics that are within the direct control of eCommerce teams. Subscription business models within eCommerce (think Dollar Shave Club, Ipsy, and BarkBox) have mushroomed across the globe for this very reason.[31]

While your business might not be ripe for recurrent regular purchase, all of the tactics deployed by subscription business models can become a very useful playbook for all eCommerce brands.

From an advertising perspective, if we know that the AOV of a new customer is $100 and we need to achieve a ROAS of 5x, then we immediately know our goal. We need to spend no more than $20 to acquire a new customer.

However, if our LTV is €250, and we need to achieve the same 5X ROAS, then we know we can compete better in the auctions with a budget of €50 to acquire each new customer.

ROAS is an incredibly useful measure of marketing contribution, as it directly links advertising performance with its impact on the company's bottom line. By increasing the ROAS, we are spending the same amount on advertising to achieve higher revenues.

Conversely, we are achieving higher contribution margins which means we will have more to invest in future marketing efforts. Benchmarking ROAS within your business channels and across your industry category is a very useful way to set and manage expectations about future growth through paid media.

At different stages of the funnel, we need to measure our ROI in different ways. For sure, we are reporting at a top level across the board on a metric such as ROAS. At the lower and sometimes middle of the funnel we are also focused on ROAS.

However, our goal in mid-funnel is to educate engaged audiences and entice them to visit our site, to purchase either today or at some future date. Therefore, ROAS is too one-dimensional for effective management of campaigns in mid-funnel. We typically focus on other metrics such as cost-per-click, cost-per-landing page view, or conversion rate.

At the earlier stage of the purchase journey, our goal is to find people who might be interested in our offering; having an itch we can scratch. We might measure clicks to our website from ad campaigns at the top of the funnel, but very often we are focused on building audiences which we can nurture through the later stages of purchase intent. Other metrics such as cost per reach, cost per video view or cost per impression are more appropriate here.

Understanding the contribution your advertising makes through the funnel and being able to effectively align daily performance metrics with financial margin considerations ensures you can **scale efficiently**. Sustainable eCommerce growth is what we're all chasing.

Maybe you've just had some nice results from lower funnel ad campaigns during a peak shopping period and have been given the mandate to scale up. You've got the wind at your back but consider your strategy for capitalizing on those early wins in the medium to longer term before you set expectations too high.

Invest wisely in paid media right through the funnel and closely align advertising with other internal marketing and sales activities. It is this holistic approach that is behind many of the most successful eCommerce growth stories we hear about today.

In the next chapters we'll examine each stage of our three-step funnel and identify practical considerations for how to nudge shoppers efficiently and effectively through their personal purchase journey.

As we navigate through the funnel we encounter the same four dimensions that we need to consider:

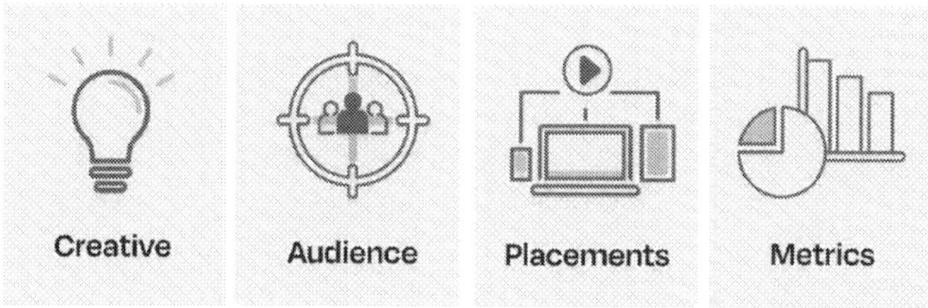

- **Creative** - creative is the single biggest contributor to sales by a specific advertising element. Nielsen, in fact, suggests that it is nearly twice as important as any other contributing factor in your advertising mix.[32]
- **Audience** - audience is the second most important dimension in your advertising strategy. Going too broad, will lead to wastage. Going too narrow, can quickly lead to lost opportunity and overly high frequencies.
- **Placements** - the context of where your creative appears before different audiences is important. Each ad platform provides a wide range of options and we need to consider the options that help us achieve the highest impact.
- **Metrics** - we all know that what gets measured gets managed. Setting the right metrics at each stage of the funnel, aligned with how we are supporting customer decision-making, ensures we are *doing* the right things.

#2 Checklist

→ Create a **customer journey map** that describes what consumers are doing, thinking, and feeling at each stage of their purchase journey.

→ Map out for **each key persona, why** they should make a change in their lives, why they should choose you, and why they should change now.

→ Identify and understand **existing key measures** at each stage of the funnel; ROAS, cost per click, cost per video view etc.

→ Clarify **marketing contribution**; the margin available for you to acquire new customers, especially in the context of lifetime value analysis.

→ Begin to **educate stakeholders** on the economic and practical necessity to invest across the funnel, to nurture consumers to maximize ROI.

#3

INSPIRING COLD AUDIENCES

My first marketing boss summarized the purpose of marketing as "satisfying customer needs profitably." Breaking that down a little more, we could suggest that a marketer's priority is to cost-efficiently engage audiences with a brand's story, educate them about the brand's offering, and convince them to buy.

Much of the storytelling behind a brand takes place at the upper end of the funnel; casting the net out wide with our unique positioning and fishing for consumers with whom our story resonates. These "cold" audiences are probably not aware of our brand and, in many instances, may not even be aware that there is a solution to the problem our products solve.

Our task at the top of the funnel is to **generate awareness and interest** to create cohorts that we can begin to nurture through our sales journey. At the upper end of the funnel, we are in story-telling mode; **inspiring people** with our unique story or our unique offering and showing how it transforms people's lives. Here, our product is not the hero. The hero is the consumer and a vision of what the future looks like, thanks to our offering.

Story-telling Creative

Since we are in story-telling mode, the optimum creative approach is typically **short-form video**. To quote Peter Field and Les Binet, "nothing builds a brand like emotion, and nothing drives emotion like video."[33] There are several reasons for this. Video gives the unique opportunity to address different senses and begin to establish an emotional connection with audiences.

Increasingly, we find ourselves choosing short-form video as the jumping off point; typically, less than 15 seconds. Very often the ad platforms themselves deliver improved performance for shorter-form video. The platforms have their own incentives for users to navigate quickly through the feed and so shorter is better for them too. In addition, identifying audiences who are inspired enough to watch our full video, but not necessarily click through to our website is a great way to **cost-effectively kick-start** the purchase journey.

Can you tell a meaningful brand story in 15 seconds or less? Definitely. Here are some great examples:

- Moen's "Buy It For Life Lessons | Oxby Faucet" (faucets). In this video, grandpa and boy are working together to fix a leaky faucet. The hero is grandpa, but all the while we're learning about how Moen transforms grandpa's life - it's easy even for grandpas and their young grandkids to install.[34]

- Domino's "New Bigger Better Pizza" (pizza). In just 10 seconds, Domino's humorously communicates one very clear message about its new bigger pizza. The ad is split 50:50 between storytelling and brand message, so in just 5 seconds, our attention is grabbed, and curiosity generated.[35]
- Bounce's "Want less static in your clothes? Bounce dryer sheets to the rescue." (fmcg). Again, in just 5 seconds, this commercial from Bounce brings emotion and clarity of message for their static prevention sheets. Worried dad looking for son Billy doesn't want to be interrupted by the "ad lady," but the humorous twist with mischievous Billy sells us in seconds.[36]
- Lens Direct's "Scratched Lens? Outdated Prescription" (apparel). Here, in 15 seconds, Lens Direct communicates the problem and the efficiency of solving the problem with very clear copy and visual storytelling. For inspiration check out this ad and more great examples of brand story-telling from the Chamber Media studio.[37]

In all of these examples, story-telling and emotion are high. The product features strongly, but is not necessarily the focal point. The focus is on the humans, **resonating with the real problems, needs and desires** of the target audience.

Push yourself, or your team, to deliver your most compelling message in the shortest time possible - ideally in less than 1-2 seconds. I'm not suggesting you create micro video ads, but you could take some inspiration from those famous one second Super Bowl ads for Master Lock[38] or Miller High Life[39].

With upper funnel videos, we are absolutely in attention-grabbing mode, so here are some top tips for how to make videos work for you, regardless of the ad channel you are using:

- **Grab Attention Early** - research consistently shows that as attention spans decrease we have less and less time to grab attention. Within the first 2 seconds you need to have captured attention.[40]
- **Get Your Brand in Early** - it is important to get your brand in early, in those first few seconds. However, we often see that when branding dominates too early, drop-offs can rise. So have it there, but subtly.
- **Works Without Audio** - 85% of Facebook video is watched without audio.[41] Ensure your video works without sound but avoid subtitles. Combine visual storytelling with short standout phrases.
- **Language Hooks** - titles and key messages that are promising knowledge ("Things to know") or need satisfaction ("What you need") have been shown to deliver higher results.[42]
- **Emotional Hooks** - consider that amongst the biggest drivers of viral video engagement are

emotion and positivity; try to ensure that your upper funnel creative tells stories close to the person.[43]

- **Simplicity** - with shorter times than ever to grab attention, keep your message and overall approach as simple as possible. Rather than cram in multiple messages in one video ad, consider developing a short series.[44]
- **Land Your Message** - once you've grabbed their attention, always retain the last few seconds to nail your message and include a call to action. Initially, we're focused on building awareness, but make it easy for those who are hooked to take the next step.

Casting the Net: Audience-Building

Hand in hand with great creative execution, is ensuring your message is presented to the right audience in the right context. The ad platforms will encourage you to go as broad as possible with reach campaigns, however, we like to **avoid spray-and-pray strategies**.

Your creative was likely developed with specific personas in mind. Let's deep dive into these personas and leverage the data we already have at our disposal to go fishing for them across multiple channels.

Interest-based Audiences

Most ad platforms today allow you to create target audiences using **interest-based** categories. These can vary from demographics, to location, to the kinds of things that people like to do, either on the platform themselves or on third-party websites.

Remember that platforms such as Facebook, Google, Microsoft (Bing, Yahoo! & LinkedIn), and Pinterest are tracking logged-in user behaviors right across the internet, so their algorithms know a lot more about individuals than you can possibly imagine.

Every eCommerce website that is advertising on these platforms, is essentially enabling the ad platforms to build incredibly detailed profiles of individuals as they traverse the web. Start with interest-based audiences by mapping out types of interests and behaviors that your own ideal persona is likely to display and then align with the options available within the ad platforms themselves.

You can undertake first-party research to identify your **audience interests**, but of course the platforms are there to help make this easier. Here are some examples:

- Facebook's Audience Insights tool enables you to identify behaviors and interests of people who have already engaged with your social profiles.

- The Google Ads Audience insights tool enables you to identify interests and purchase intent of audiences you may have in your remarketing lists or who have already converted.

- Pinterest's Audience Insights feature enables you to understand better what your existing and potential audiences are interested in based on their engagements with your pins, both paid and organic, and pins saved from your website.

Another great place to go is your Google Analytics Audience report. In addition to everything you might expect such as location, demographics, and devices, you can access data on the general and shopping interests of your audiences (affinity categories), plus the categories where Google determines the audiences are "more likely to be ready to purchase products or services."

Intentful Audiences

Leveraging the ad platforms' data to go fishing for **audiences displaying purchase intent** in your category is a very important tactic for improving the efficiency of advertising at the top of the funnel. Layering in intent on top of other targeting options has been shown to deliver significant improvements in video ad performance.

A recent study by IPSOS/Google analyzed the use of different targeting options for YouTube ads amongst 1,800 U.S. adults.[45] It discovered that when intent is used as a targeting option, in addition to demographic targeting, there was considerable lift in ad effectiveness.

- Ad recall increased by 32%
- Awareness increased by 167%
- Consideration increased by 267%
- Purchase intent increased by 100%

In addition, the study demonstrated that for skippable ad

placements, the skip rate reduces from 61% to 51% when intent was used instead of demographics for targeting. There's an immediate ten percentage point reduction in ad spend waste, simply by choosing an optimum targeting strategy.

Audience-Matching

If you already have a customer base, then leveraging the platforms' **audience-matching capabilities** can be a powerful way to find people with interests and behaviors that are like your customers'. These are sometimes called "lookalike" audiences.

A "1% lookalike audience," for example, represents the other 1% of the population that is most like your own customers. So, if the available population you are targeting is 10 million, a 1% lookalike audience is the segment of 100,000 people in that population that displays behaviors most similar to your existing customer base.

This is a great place to start. If your initial audience is not big enough, you can go broader and use a 2% or 3% lookalike. Remember that the broader you go, the less "similar" the audience will be with your own and the poorer they are likely to perform for you.

Jubly Umph is an Australian eCommerce business that sells art, jewelry, and other accessories. When it first considered expanding beyond Australia, they leveraged lookalike audiences within the Facebook environment to find audiences in other markets with similar attributes to their existing Australian customer base. This approach yielded 3.1x higher return on ad spend when compared with interest-based audiences.[46]

Inspiring Video Placements

Since we prefer video as the optimum format for communicating our brand story, when considering which platforms to use we focus on those who do the best job of presenting our video creative to the right audiences. All the major advertising platforms provide some form of video advertising infrastructure. We tend to take an agnostic view on specific platforms, basing our decisions on the channels that deliver the highest levels of meaningful engagement with our creative storyline.

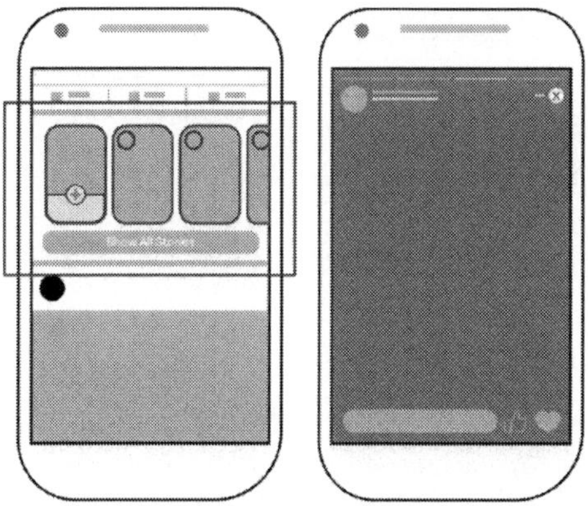

Figure 14 Immersive full-screen ads

We prefer environments where our video is presented naturally to the user, with as little distraction as possible and with low levels of enforced behaviors. The story-ad formats in Facebook, Instagram, and Snapchat are great examples of this. With story-ads, 100% of the mobile screen is dedicated to you and your video creative.

Video-pins in Pinterest are an often-forgotten ad format that can address inspiration-seekers who align with your target persona.

And let's not forget YouTube video ads, the second largest search engine on the platform, where the words "how to" combined with topics such as home improvement, beauty, and cooking are growing by 70% per annum.[47]

YouTube provides probably the broadest selection of video ad placements and recommends 6-second "Bumper" for brand awareness and reach. These are ads which are non-skippable and appear before, during or after a video. We're a little wary of non-skippable ads, so we do like "discovery" more, which appear alongside other videos or in search results and we're only charged when someone actually chooses to watch our ad.

At this point in the funnel, we want to work with platforms that enable us to create audiences based on those who have engaged most fully with our video. Facebook, Instagram, and Pinterest do this nicely by allowing us to build audiences based on those who have watched specific percentages of your video.

Start with 100% and work back from there. The "video remarketing" feature within the Google Ads environment enables us to build audiences based on a wide range of engagement types with our linked YouTube channel and ads content. It's a bonus to drive click-throughs, but our focus right now is on engagement.

One word of caution, coming from painful experience: consider actively **excluding placements where users are forced to watch videos** to complete a task or earn a credit.

One culprit can be the reward videos on the Facebook Audience Network. This placement forces a user to watch a video ad to gain some benefit within an unrelated environment. Facebook will include this placement in your mix by default and if you are optimizing your campaigns for 100% view-through, then you'll end up with the platform automatically dumping your spend into these placements and the audience that we've created will be relatively useless.

Other formats from YouTube, Google and Facebook which force users to watch video either before or during an editorial or user-generated video can make us fall foul of the same false positive audience identification. Building audiences based on users who have been forced to watch your video will not necessarily deliver higher quality engagement lower down the funnel. Strongly consider whether to include placements that are unskippable or provide the wrong incentives for someone to engage with our unique story.

If you do choose a platform or placements that forces a user to watch several seconds of our video before proceeding to do what they really wanted to do, then be aware that our story-telling task is suddenly more difficult for several reasons:

First, context is key here. They're being asked to do something they don't want to do, so the few seconds they do watch need to overcome their negative emotional disposition and then also convince them to keep watching.

Furthermore, our engagement metrics will be greatly skewed - just because someone was forced to watch a specific duration of your video creative. Therefore, this placement type doesn't provide any reliable indication of their usefulness to us further along the purchase journey. I'd much rather have fewer people to talk to if they are people who have willingly engaged with my story.

Engagement Metrics

The goal at the upper end of the funnel is to **create engaged audiences as efficiently as possible** which can be addressed later with follow-on messages to nurture them through the next stages of the purchase journey.

At this stage, we are not trying to drive sales per se; small volumes will certainly be achieved at this stage for sure, but we're still in storytelling/inspiration mode. (Of course, we are very happy when audiences click-through and proceed to purchase.)

By using video as our creative anchor, we can build audiences from those who have watched a certain percentage of our video story and ignore those who rapidly thumbed past it. For example, we may reach 100,000 unique individuals with our 15" video across the Facebook/Instagram family, but if only 10,000 watch 100% of the video, and a further 20,000 watched just 75%, we might want to focus on creating an **engaged** audience initially from those 30,000 combined.

Our measure of efficiency is a blend of achieving the **lowest cost per view-through with the highest click-through rate**. A "view-through" is typically defined as a user having watched the shorter of 100% or (usually) 15 seconds of a video ad. Rather than setting "video-views" as the objective of your campaign, set "view-through" as the optimization objective to ensure maximum effectiveness.

While we are not seeking to drive any specific behavior other than for them to watch our video, click-through rate will be a useful secondary indicative measure of a higher level of engagement with our brand and can be a useful metric to optimize against. The click-through rate also enables us to quickly identify where ad platforms have presented our messages to **irrelevant audiences** and possibly forced them to watch for some ulterior motive.

Getting access to these upper funnel metrics is relatively straightforward. Since all the activity here is taking place within the ad platform, then the stats are best sourced directly from the ad platform's own reports. As always, we should ensure we are comparing apples with apples by aligning the filters on reports within each platform.

We need to be sure that how we measure a video view in one platform is the same as in all others. So, for example, a 100% view of a six-second ad on YouTube should not be counted or costed in the same way as a 100% view of a fifteen-second video ad on Instagram. If we can't align the data to be consistent, then at least we need to be aware that our ROI metrics for upper funnel campaigns are different in each channel.

For many brands, it can seem difficult or costly to create video for inspiring cold audiences. I can only reiterate the value of this investment and the efficiency that it will help to drive throughout the funnel. For those who simply can't use video or want to use a mix of formats, combining reach and impression metrics with engagement metrics can be a powerful way to ensure you are investing in the right places. For example, prioritizing campaigns that drive the **lowest cost per impression and the highest click-through-rate** is a great way to ensure you are investing both in higher value audience cohorts.

When starting out, more of our overall spend will be focused on the upper funnel. However, over time, this proportion will reduce considerably. We see highly effective strategies committing between 10-20% of budget on an ongoing basis into awareness campaigns. As a rule of thumb, upper funnel budgets increase when the volume of audiences at lower funnel stages are too small and the efficiency of ad spend in those stages are disimproving. Balancing budget across your funnel for maximum cost-effectiveness is a constant task for today's marketer, and one thankfully where help is at hand as we'll see later.

#3 Checklist

→ Develop **short-form video** which seeks to engage target audiences with the story of how your offer can transform lives.

→ Learn how to **develop effective video** by grabbing attention early, keeping it simple, ensuring it works without text, and landing it.

→ Start **building engaged audiences** by leveraging the capabilities of the platforms using interest-based, intentful, and audience matches.

→ Focus on **immersive placements**, where the ad platforms can provide the richest environment to inspire audiences with our great stories.

→ Consider **avoiding certain placements** that force users to watch full videos and thus, provide you with false positive engagement metrics.

→ Narrow in on the goal of **creating engaged audiences** based on those who've actively and voluntarily watched our stories.

→ Effectively measure **cost per view-through** (100% of a 15" video) and commence by assigning between 10-20% of budget.

#4

EDUCATING WARM AUDIENCES

Warm audiences are those that have some awareness of our brand or have demonstrated interest in our offering. We're not sure yet if they're ready to purchase, as their engagement with us so far has been light. They may have engaged with our video, perhaps visited, or liked our social media instances, or may have checked out our web store or app.

Our goal is to nudge warm audiences further through the purchase process by educating them about the unique features and benefits of our products. We are moving from more emotional engagement to rational engagement. We're assuming that the shopper is in research mode and probably checking out alternative solutions, including our competitors. The product starts to come into sharper focus, and we have to highlight all of the ways in which our offering is the best available.

While at all stages of the funnel we are seeking to drive

customers to our eCommerce store, here, the call-to-action (CTA) becomes much more prominent. We will start to use more dynamic creative formats to better match our messaging with individual shoppers' preferences and behaviors. As we seek to efficiently drive engaged customers to our website, we fine-tune the channels, audiences, and creative formats that can deliver us the most valuable cohorts.

Creative that Educates

With warm audiences, we're putting our message in front of consumers who have already demonstrated some interest in our brand or product, and we can expect that we have more than just a couple of seconds to snatch their attention. These shoppers are in research mode and are looking for more detail.

The role of advertising is to provide the briefest summary of the key features and benefits of our product to entice shoppers to dig deeper. Two very popular creative formats that work well here are longer form video and interactive ads. Both formats give us the opportunity to provide more detail to engaged audiences and support their appetite for additional detail.

a. Longer Form Video

By **longer form video,** we typically mean somewhere between 30 and 120 seconds, depending on how complex our product is. The platforms themselves don't love longer form video ads, but time and again we see higher conversion rates at this stage in the funnel when used appropriately.

In the video, we may reiterate our emotional messages, however, the focus of these videos is to highlight key or unique features and benefits.

Here are some great examples:

- Dollar Shave Club (personal care) - this explainer ad from Dollar Shave Club is probably one of the best examples of combining humor with product information and addressing purchase objections head-on.[48]

- Tulane's Closet (pets) - this ad leverages a practical explainer video format to showcase many of the key features and benefits in 60 seconds. The video ad doesn't need to be of high production quality to be effective.[49]

- Knorr (food) - recipes and cooking demonstrations are great ways to showcase food products in action; providing both inspiration and demonstrating how easy it is to incorporate this ingredient into a delicious meal. [50]

If you're struggling to create video, the physical real estate made available to advertising within ad platforms or on publisher websites is often quite limited. And so, **interactive ads** enable users to access more information within the ad unit beyond an initial static or video panel.

The three most interesting formats are carousel ads, collection ads, and augmented reality (AR) ads.

b. Carousel Ads

Multi-frame ads like "Carousel" ads on Facebook[51] or Google's "Gallery" [52] - provide multiple frames which a user can swipe through in order to see different features or dig deeper into a brand story. A carousel will typically contain between 3 and 10 frames. Each frame gives you the opportunity to deliver a different message.

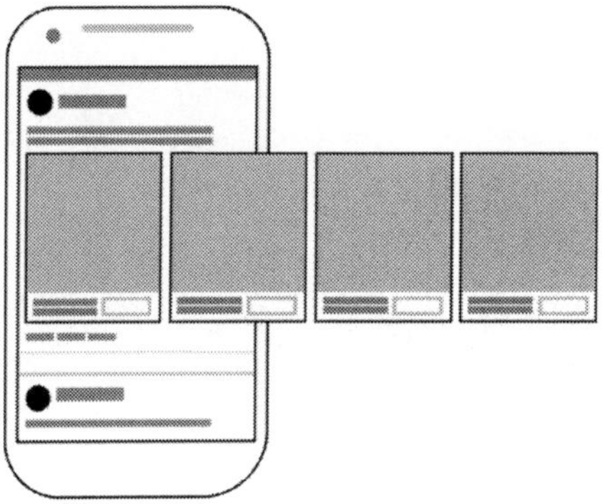

Figure 15 Carousel ads

When considering how to make the best use of carousel ads, we like to think of them as the storyboard for your story, with a beginning, middle, and end. The first frame sets up the story; enticing users to find out more. The middle frames provide the substance, highlighting key features and benefit messages. The final frame brings it all together; tying it up with a conclusion that directs users to your brand store.

c. Collection Ads

Collection Ads enable you to go one step further, joining the dots between discovery elements such as video or imagery and your product catalog. In the Facebook and Instagram environment, the collection ad format presents the user with a hero video or image, followed by a grid highlighting related products from your catalog.[53]

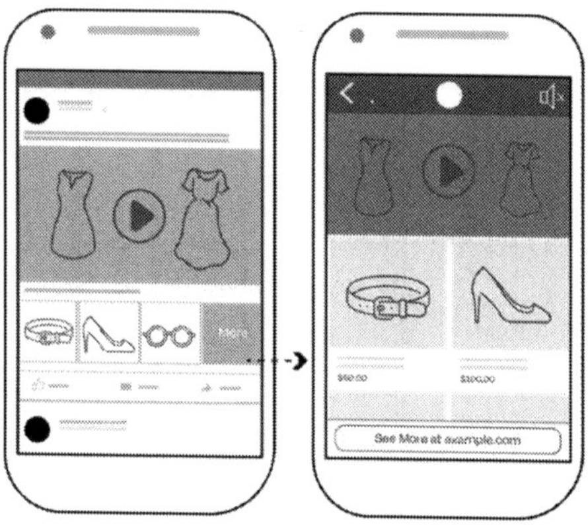

Figure 16 Combined video and shopping ads

Snapchat provides a similar collection ad feature, overlaying full-screen video with four tappable product images.[54] Even YouTube, which has been notoriously slow to the eCommerce game, has now introduced shoppable tiles below video ads.[55] In all cases, the product tiles seamlessly take shoppers to the relevant product page on your website.

In the U.S., companies that have checkout-enabled Instagram and Facebook accounts can facilitate purchases directly in-app on these platforms. Enabling checkout within your Facebook Ads environment removes significant friction for the growing volumes of especially younger shoppers who are making purchases directly within the social media apps.[56]

d. Instant Experiences

Instant Experiences (formerly known as Canvas Ads) are a format unique to Instagram and Facebook that enable users to expand an ad out into an immersive full screen brand experience within the platform.[57] A user clicks on a normal ad unit and within a full-frame environment can watch videos and photos, swipe through carousels, tilt to pan and explore lifestyle images with tagged products.

This format enables you to present a comprehensive overview of your brand offering directly within the ad platform, reducing the friction of taking users to your website. This is a great format for educating audiences without them needing to leave Facebook or Instagram. Of course, you ultimately want to drive clicks and conversions and you can set these as objectives when creating the ad.

e. Augmented Reality (AR) Ads

AR ads, such as those commonly used on Snapchat and Facebook, bring products to life in a meaningful and often fun way. Until recently, these formats were out of reach for most brands, however, brilliant companies such as Plop, EyeKandy, or Blippar are making it easy and affordable for eCommerce stores to try this format. One of Plop's clients, Swyft, a furniture retailer, was quickly able to achieve a consistent 24-25x ROAS from using AR ads within their Facebook ads mix.[58]

Check out some other companies using AR within Snapchat, such as Cleary (optical try-on)[59], Ponds (beauty cleanser)[60], and Nisnas (clothing)[61].

Italian make-up brand We Make-up leveraged Facebook AR ads to try on different shades of liquid lipstick through a face filter. These ads delivered a direct performance hit with a 28% lift in purchases during the first month.[62]

Great Copy Converts

At the mid and lower stages of the funnel, **copy** is a critical ingredient in our ads to be combined with our awesome creative. The types of placements we tend to use in lower funnel stages are text-rich, since we have more detailed and precise messages to communicate. There are typically three types of copy to consider:

1. **The Headline** - this is the key hook or offer that must grab attention and combined with the creative image/video, entice the audience to delve deeper. Understanding how many characters a user will see from your headline before clicking the "see more" link is a must to ensure your core message is visible 100% of the time.

2. **The Body** - depending on the placement this could be a longer or shorter piece of text, but it is where you get to call out specific features, benefits, and offer details. In a carousel ad format, each piece of body text should align with one simple message conveyed in the image frame.

3. **The Call to Action (CTA)** - the button or link that typically sits alongside your body text. Choose a button that signifies purchase intent, like "buy now" and you're likely to see lower clicks but higher conversions from those clicks. Choose a button that signifies research, such as "learn more" and you're likely to see higher click-throughs, but perhaps lower conversions.

Nurturing Warm Audiences

Warm audiences are those that have established some connection with your brand or who have demonstrated **initial purchase intent** in your product category. Warm audiences have indicated somehow that they are more likely to be interested in your brand and offerings, so we must take a different approach with them than with cold audiences. Thankfully, the various ad platforms provide a multitude of ways in which to narrow in on these warm audiences.

We've already seen how we can build audiences from those who have meaningfully engaged in our upper funnel campaigns; **voluntarily watched our videos** with demonstrable interest, watching at least 75% of our 15" or

100% of our 6" video ads. Consider including those who have engaged with your **organic social activities** - watched a video, followed a page, liked, or shared a post - in the mix as well.

When hunting for warm audiences, we tend to include those who have **visited our website**, but not yet progressed through our purchase funnel. They may have visited a landing page or a product detail page, but not yet added a product to the basket. They've clearly displayed a propensity to engage with our brand, but still need to be convinced to take the next step.

Where you have implemented an **email collection** mechanism on your landing pages, these can be great ways to build audience lists of people who can be messaged elsewhere. Collect the appropriate consent and you can upload these data points to the ad platforms for more personalized targeting. This approach is becoming increasingly important as cookies and pixel-tracking come under pressure across the industry.

Connecting **real customer data points** with ad platforms helps you overcome browser and app tracking issues, and ensures you are connecting with real people in your ads. Solutions for this are available from all the major ad platforms:

- **Facebook Ads** allows you to create a "custom audience" from a customer list.
- **Google Ads** enables you to create a "customer list" from your first-party data.

- **Pinterest Ads** provides a "customer list audience" from email and mobile data.
- **Amazon Ads** solution for list-building is called "advertiser hashed audiences".
- **Snap Ads** offers this capability through it's "audience match" facility.

When using customer lists, be conscious that the "match-rate" between your own list and the ad platforms is likely to be well below 100%. For every 100 customer emails or phone numbers you upload, you might reasonably expect a 30-40% match. If you get lucky, it could be much higher.

The platforms typically need a minimum of 1,000 data points in each uploaded list and, clearly, the larger your list size, the more effective this approach will be. The additional benefit here is that all the platforms allow you to find *similar* audiences on the platform based on your customer list, which is a great way to build out upper and middle funnel audiences.

At this stage of the funnel, we also seek out purchase intent signals from properties using data that we don't necessarily own. **Long-tail keywords** are the phrases that consumers use typically when they are closer to the point of purchase or when using voice search. They are often more specific and contain more words than higher-funnel search terms.

Advertising against long-tail keyword targeting on the search platforms can prove to be a cost-effective way to get your message in front of in-market consumers who are actively researching. Long-tail keywords will often be less competitive and have been demonstrated to deliver customers with higher purchase intent.[63]

The Custom Intent Audiences feature within Google Ads now enables you to target users with video ads on YouTube based on their search activity on Google Search. This is a potentially useful way for you to avoid the madness of the PPC search auctions for important keywords and address users with engaging creative in an environment such as YouTube. 80% of shoppers switch between Google and YouTube when researching and 55% start on Google and then head across to YouTube to learn more before purchasing.[64]

Middle Funnel Placements

The best mid-funnel platforms are those that can help us sharpen our targeting based on audiences who have engaged with our brand or that can assist us in establishing clear purchase intent. In addition, we want to capture audiences where they are likely to have longer dwell time and are not simply flicking through video reels.

By working with the same channels, we choose for upper funnel campaigns, we can leverage the native capabilities within each channel to build out warm audience pools. However, often the placements that are good at upper funnel are not as effective further down the funnel. Therefore, we need to ensure we are able to remarket to website visitors to, regardless of where they came from.

All of the major platforms provide **remarketing capabilities** based on either the presence of their pixel on your website, server-side integrations, or customer list data integration. From day one, it is therefore important to decide which platforms you're going to use at this stage in the funnel, as you'll want to ensure your tagging and data integration is set up for success. Once this is in place, you will, in most cases, be able to create those custom audiences within the ad platform based on the types of action that users have taken on your website.

Our mid-funnel audiences are likely to be those that have visited perhaps only one or two pages and haven't progressed through your purchase funnel. They may have arrived on your landing page and clicked through to several product pages, but not yet added anything to their basket.

Initial purchase intent has been established, but we have more work to do to bring to the next stage. When building these audiences based on website events, we can include, for example, users who visited your home page or landing page and actively exclude those who visited a specific product page or added a product to their shopping basket.

The exact placements selected will vary depending on the creative format used and the capabilities of each platform to use them in specific locations. Longer form videos, for example, will be less appropriate as a pre-roll to an editorial or user-generated content. Let's **not force users to engage with our message** when they have a very specific activity in mind.

The Facebook feed can be a great placement for carousel ads, since audiences tend to scroll through this particular feed at a slower pace. The quality of engagement can be improved as their frame of mind is less intentional and perhaps even looking for inspiration.

Many of the platforms suggest using **automated placements** to start, and then optimizing based on early performance indicators. This means that we give the platforms the greatest opportunity to find the right placement for our creative and audience mix.

Ad formats and placements from different platforms that we've seen working well at this stage of the funnel include:

- **Facebook** - video ads, "carousel" ads, "collection" ads, marketplace ads
- **Instagram** - video ads, "carousel" ads, "collection" ads, checkout in-app
- **Google** - long tail keywords, category keywords, competitor keywords
- **YouTube** – "TrueView for Action" ads, custom intent ads, "collection" ads
- **Pinterest** – "collection" ads
- **Microsoft** - long tail keywords, competitor keywords
- **Snapchat** – "lens" ads, "collection" ads

Traffic Metrics

We often call mid-funnel campaigns "traffic" campaigns, since our primary goal is to deliver engaged visitors to our website who, hopefully, have a high propensity to convert.

Our primary metric is **cost-per-click (CPC)** and we will optimize our campaign creatives, audiences, and bidding strategies to deliver more quality visitors with a lower cost-per-click.

The main objective of these campaigns is not to drive conversions; however, we do expect some conversions to materialize. In fact, **the ratio of conversions to clicks** is a very useful metric of the performance of a traffic campaign. We therefore take conversion rate (CVR) into account when making decisions about a traffic campaign's performance.

Very often, we will find that some types of campaigns deliver high volumes of traffic that doesn't convert. This can be for any number of reasons - the audience is not quite right, the creative is out of sync with our product offering, or the platform's own algorithms are favoring volume over quality. Digging deeper into campaigns with lower CVRs can be a very useful exercise in identifying specific campaign dynamics that need to be adjusted or removed.

Aligning data across platforms becomes more difficult as we move down the funnel. While cost-per-click data is comparable across ad channels, **identifying the true contribution to conversions to each channel is more complex**. Individual ad channels cannot identify the other contributing factors in a conversion.

A customer clicks on a Pinterest ad and after several days makes a purchase, having perhaps visited the site several more times in between. Pinterest will report that conversion against a specific ad and user. So too will any other ad channel where that customer interacted with an ad prior to purchase. And so, the double counting begins.

This is an important stage in the funnel and will command a much **greater proportion of the budget**. Over time, somewhere between 20-60% of ad budget assigned to educating and drawing customers to your website is about the right range for an eCommerce business.

Early on, your spend will be at the higher end of the range and will decrease over time. Over-invest and you'll spread your budget too thinly, starving upper and lower funnel stages. Under-invest and you won't build enough volume required to drive lower funnel efficiencies.

#4 Checklist

→ Develop **longer form video** (30-120 seconds) which bring the benefits and features of the product to the fore.

→ Implement **multi-frame ads** such as carousels or galleries, to highlight a range of product benefits in a single ad unit.

→ Trial **other interactive ad formats,** such as ads that combine video with product catalog or AR to enable users see your product in context.

→ Carefully script **copy** that is optimized for the various placements available with key message visible up front, benefits highlighted and clear calls to action.

→ Build **warm audience cohorts** from those who have engaged in video stories and by leveraging customer lists to find similar audiences.

→ Choose **automated placements** initially but narrow in on those that deliver the highest volumes of quality traffic at the lowest cost.

→ Measure quality traffic based on a **blend of cost-per-click and conversion rate**, with an investment of between 20-60% of overall budget.

#5

CONVINCING HOT AUDIENCES

Hot audiences have **demonstrated strong purchase intent but** have not completed a transaction. They may be new or returning website visitors, repeat or lapsed customers, or shoppers who have shown interest in specific products and perhaps progressed through our purchase funnel, but exited without converting.

You can expect as many as seven out of every ten shoppers who add a product to their cart will abandon that cart.[65] On the assumption that our CRO strategy is robust, our premise as advertisers is that this cohort is a rich hunting ground for conversion campaigns. And let's not forget, customer segments who've purchased from us previously; we want to tactically approach them at times when they are likely to make their next purchase from us.

Advertising's role is to support and complement the broader team's ongoing CRO and CRM activities. At this stage in the funnel, we know that shoppers are interested in specific products and yet there has been some blockage to purchase. Now we focus on personalizing the message with the product as the absolute hero of every message. We need to help consumers overcome lingering purchase objections and, hopefully, convince them to complete their intended purchase right now.

Conversion-focused Creatives

For shoppers who have demonstrated purchase intent towards specific products, by far the most effective advertising message at our disposal is a **reminder of the product they were interested in, coupled with compelling reasons to purchase now**. At this stage in the funnel, your product catalog comes into its own.

Whereas "collection" ads help shoppers navigate from inspirational moments to products they might be interested in, dynamic "catalog" ads drive shoppers back to the specific product they actively considered purchasing. Combining product personalization with compelling reasons to purchase now, such as time-bound offers, is the perfect recipe for success with conversion campaigns.

Dynamic catalog ads or "dynamic product ads" as they are sometimes called, enable you to harness the power of the ad platforms' algorithms to present the right product to the right customer at the right time.

Before you begin, you'll need to have the platform's tracking pixel on your product page and have connected your product catalog with the ad platform. Then, depending on how you configure your dynamic catalog ad, the ad platform will show a user an image of the product they viewed on your web store the next time they are on the platform. Typically, additional information can be overlaid with the product image, such as title, description, call to action, price and any discounts that are live. Because your live catalog is in sync with the ad platform, shoppers will only be shown products that are currently in stock.

Spanish shoe brand Espadrij L'Originale attributed a 4.8x improvement in ROAS on Facebook to the introduction of dynamic product ads, in combination with carousel and collection ads for their summer sale, enabling them to personalize the product displayed to a customer after visiting their website.[66]

Where you don't have your catalog connected with the ad platforms and to compensate for those users who have blocked ad cookies, it is worthwhile running **dynamic creative ads** in parallel. Dynamic creative ads, enable you to manually upload and input multiple variants of different assets (text, imagery, video, calls-to-action) to the ad platforms and then leverage the platform's algorithms to present the right combination of variants to each user in turn. So, while the product message is not personalized to the user, the combination of creative components is optimized towards individuals based on the desired outcome.

UK fashion retailer JD Williams switched from using static collection and carousel ads to dynamic versions of these ads and attributed a 21% immediate uplift in incremental conversions to the introduction of personalization.[67] Another UK retailer, Topps Tiles, saw a similar level of improvement (29% improved CPA) using the equivalent dynamic "responsive search ads" in Google.[68]

Figure 17 Responsive Ads Automatically Adjust to Placement

Both dynamic catalog ads and **dynamic creative ads** can also be used effectively further up the funnel for prospecting to broader audiences. Here, the platform's machine learning takes control and presents the right combination of assets to users they assess to be interested in your specific products or who will respond better to different creative variants. Remember that cost efficiencies will typically be lower when prospecting with dynamic catalog ads than when you are personalizing based on already-displayed purchase intent on your store.

With so many creative options available right across the

funnel, we need to develop a systematic approach to testing and optimizing different variants. No two eCommerce businesses are the same, and so there is no substitute for gaining your own insights about how consumers react to your brand and product messages. Creative and copy are an investment you must be prepared to make but can quickly demonstrate results that fully justifies that investment.

Narrowing in on Hot Audiences

Hot audiences are those who have demonstrated a high level of purchase intent either on our own site or elsewhere. In principle, with the right data infrastructure and catalog integrations in place we can make it easy for the ad platforms to do what they do best - present appropriate messages in a timely manner to the best audiences.

Right across the funnel, but particularly at the lower end of the funnel, aligning **offers, along with urgency and scarcity** messages, with audience segments is vital to achieving our business objectives. Especially when advertising within social environments, we tend to consider audiences in at least three buckets:

1. **Shoppers who never bought from us before** - are shoppers who we have warmed up and we want to provide them with a not-to-be-missed time-based limited offer that they may fear losing out on unless they click-through now.

2. **Recent customers** - are those who've bought from us in the recent past and we want to increase their average

order value. Providing exclusive offers based on basket size to loyal customers is a great way to grow repeat purchase value.

3. **Lapsed customers** – these customers have purchased from us previously, so are aware of who we are, but need something special to reignite purchase behavior. Here, we might lead with an unbeatable win-back offer which can't be found elsewhere.

Much of our lower funnel audience-building could be summarized as **creating and maintaining efficient remarketing lists**, including, and excluding segments as appropriate. We will typically be as granular as possible about the purchase journey, enabling us to prioritize the most down-stream conversion events. A typical purchase pipeline might look something like this:

-> Product Page View

-> Add to Basket

-> View Basket

-> Initiate Checkout

-> Payment Initiated

-> Payment Complete

Our first advertising priority will, for example, initially **focus on the cohort who initiated payment,** but didn't complete it. Second priority are those who started to checkout but didn't proceed past this step. Then, those who added a product to their basket, viewed their basket, but didn't proceed to the checkout. And so on. In this way we ensure that the greatest investment is always into those cohorts with the highest conversion propensity.

Email marketing lists are beneficial here, as the work we put in to creating meaningful outbound campaigns can be leveraged within paid media. An effective purchase journey usually starts by capturing email and other contact details, so that our automated outbound triggers can kick-in.

These tactics and messages can be mirrored cost-effectively in paid media channels. With the right level of consent secured, uploading hashed contact details to the platform and segmenting them based on product interest or funnel stage, provides rich information which can be used to effectively present messages in ad platforms, in parallel to email outreach.

At the lower end of the funnel, we are also likely to consider **re-engaging with previous customers** to encourage repeat purchase activities and reactivate lapsed customers. Recency, Frequency & Monetary (RFM) analysis of your customer base will provide useful data sets for conversion-focused marketing.

Anne is the Marketing Manager at a national bookstore chain who faced what felt like an insurmountable challenge: to take on Amazon and Book Depository and grow their eCommerce book sales. We quickly identified that one of Anne's most valuable assets was a well-structured database of customers who had previously purchased online.

Combining RFM analysis with purchase category history, we were able to create audience lists based on whether an individual had bought, for example, a fiction crime thriller and when their last purchase was. Lapsed crime fiction customers were targeted in paid media with a win-back offer, while irregular purchasers were enticed back with updates on the latest releases, they might be interested in.

A complementary approach is to consider implementing a **Customer Data Platform (CDP)** to unify data from across all of your marketing and other platforms in order to enable customer segmentation and timing of offers and messages to customers. CDPs are designed to take the hassle out of customer data management, by automating the processes of data collection, profile unification, segmentation. and activation. Big organizations hire teams of database administrators and marketing analysts to figure this stuff out.

My friend, David Dunne whose company, Velocidi, provides an AI-driven CDP solution, is committed to the belief that machine-learning in the hands of advertisers can help us better identify which of the 50% in ad dollars is being "wasted."

Apparel brand, Figleaves, is a client of David's, who uses their own hosted CDP to segment their customer base and automate audience-building. In one test, they were able to demonstrate how a "likely buyers" audience could improve ROAS 6.9x compared to the "unlikely buyers" segment.[69] Undoubtedly, better control and use of our own data to inform advertising strategies is a very powerful approach and likely to significantly improve efficiencies.

A key tactic we've deployed for many eCommerce brands is experimenting with the **remarketing windows**. Typically, 28-30 days is standard - targeting people equally who have deeply engaged with our site at any time in the past month. However, recency is a very strong indicator of purchase intention, especially at peak shopping times.

Therefore, developing campaign segments that give higher priority to those who have visited, for example, in the past 1-2 days can yield significantly higher return than spreading investment evenly across longer lookback windows.

The optimum remarketing window will depend on the nature of your offering and the average purchase cycle length. Experiment with different durations and find the right balance for your store.

Conversion-focused Placements

All ad platforms are not equal in the world of eCommerce, especially when it comes to converting in-market audiences. Many platforms, having seen the explosion in eCommerce globally, have invested in infrastructure and formats that are eCommerce-friendly. Others, Twitter being a prime example, have remarkably stayed away from offering specific features addressing the needs of product-led businesses.

Even, YouTube which was relatively late to the eCommerce party, only introduced shoppable ads in 2020. One of the most exciting developments as I write this is the eCommerce focus from TikTok which promises to bring online stores direct access to whole new market segments. Let's list out the obvious, and maybe some not so obvious platforms to consider.

We've known forever that **search intent** is a great way to find people who are likely to buy your product. The problem with that is *everyone* knows this. Therefore, while shopping campaigns on platforms such as Google and Microsoft (Bing and Yahoo!) *can* deliver brilliant results, very often these auctions are extremely competitive.

Our contacts in Google's eCommerce department, tell us that even smaller eCommerce brands spending as little as $150 per month could expect ROAS of 4x from Google Shopping campaigns. This is okay, but for many of these types of returns are simply too low, especially if you've invested in building audiences further up the funnel. To reach a minimum of, for example, 5x ROAS across our funnel, we need to be delivering typically at least 10-15x ROAS in our lower funnel conversion campaigns.

The Google Merchant Center and Microsoft Merchant Center are essential building blocks for your shopping campaigns, but be vigilant for the race to the bottom in terms of price and commoditization that can occur in such comparison environments, where there is little opportunity to differentiate on anything other than price.

As a retailer selling third-party products or with a drop-shipping business model, you can expect the search auctions to be highly competitive in most product categories. We've even seen direct-to-consumer brands walk away from shopping campaigns as often their retail partners are willing to bid higher and seem capable of undercutting them in these environments.

The great benefit of shopping ads on these platforms is that your product data is used to determine when a product is shown based on a shopper's purchase intent.

In the Google environment, different ad placements can include, for example:

- **Product Shopping ads.** These are automatically created based on the product data that you submit in the Merchant Center and contain such details as image, title, price, and your store or business name.

- **Showcase Shopping ads.** You'll create these in Google Ads by grouping related products together. That way people can compare several of your products and click the right one from a specific product category.

- **Local inventory ads.** These ads use feed data provided from local inventory ads, showcasing your products to nearby shoppers to engage users on the Google Display Network, and help drive traffic to your local store.

In 2018, Google removed the tagline "don't be evil" from its corporate identity and communications.[70] Google is not an evil company; however, the practice of **competitor brand search advertising** is certainly an unnecessary evil in the industry. Thanks to this practice from Google, many brands feel compelled to spend money on pay-per-click advertising when someone searches for their own brand in Google.

If you do feel compelled to spend money **advertising**

against your own brand terms, treat this investment very separately from everything else and maintain the lowest investment possible to protect your brand. Do a great job upper funnel, and, hopefully, most people will skip all your competitors advertising against your brand. If you believe there has been a trademark infringement, make a complaint to Google.[71]

While more and more eCommerce platforms such as Shopify, Big Commerce, and WooCommerce make it easy for you to export your product catalog to various ad platforms, we sometimes end up using **catalog integration services**, such as Channable or FeedOptimise, which simplify the process.

A single integration with Channable, for example, means you can make your catalog available seamlessly across dozens of ad platforms, including Facebook (including Instagram), Google (including YouTube), DoubleClick (programmatic display and video ad buying), Microsoft (including Bing & Yahoo!), Pinterest, and Snapchat.

Stepping beyond the shopping-focused environment, we love that many of these other platforms present our product messages to relevant audiences in rich media environments.

An honorable mention must go to Amazon Advertising as a proxy for **advertising within marketplaces,** such as Walmart, Ebay, and Etsy. 49% of online product searches now start directly within Amazon, therefore, it is no surprise that eCommerce brands are looking at it and other marketplaces more deeply.[72] While it has been possible to purchase sponsored listings on Amazon for many years, a comprehensive advertising offering from Amazon is relatively new thanks to several acquisitions, most notably the purchase of Sizmek in 2019.

Today, you can not only promote your product or brand listing on Amazon itself, but you can promote and drive **traffic to your own website** through Amazon's DSP (Demand-side Platform) display advertising feature. This feature is currently limited to Amazon sellers but offers a potentially powerful method for finding new customers with high purchase intent and driving them to your own website. Remember, that Amazon's unique strength is that its algorithms really do know which products customers are actively researching right now.

And finally, **influencer marketing** is not to be ignored at the lower end of the funnel. Influencers are individuals who have a dedicated social following and are viewed as experts within their niche. Influencers drive sales.[73] In fact, according to Twitter, 49% of consumers rely on recommendations from influencers in purchase decisions.[74]

While we might be more likely to use influencers at upper funnel stages, using affiliate solutions is an easy way to harness the power of influencers with ROI baked in. Affiliate marketing platforms such as GrowthHero, AWIN, CJ Affiliate, and Rakuten make it easy for eCommerce brands to have their products showcased by YouTube, Instagram & TikTok influencers and bloggers on a CPA (Cost Per Acquisition) basis.

This approach ensures that you remain in full control of your influencer marketing investment, only paying when sales are delivered. You may also choose to use a hybrid model, paying a fixed media fee together with a performance element tracked by an appropriate affiliate platform or even by using dedicated discount codes.

I particularly like the solution used by U.S. retailer Macy's from TVPage, enabling shoppable product overlays on video created by influencers and superfans. During the Covid-19 pandemic, eCommerce brands are experiencing sales revenues grow by 300% through influencer-created video.[75]

As I write, we are starting to see TikTok roll out features for eCommerce. Included is a new tool that lets influencers share links to products and earn commissions on any sales. This, combined with livestreaming shopping, as a millennial's version of TV shopping, promises to bring TikTok to the fore of eCommerce ad strategies over the coming years.

Conversion Metrics

At the bottom of the funnel, we are absolutely focused on ROI. Our key metric here is **Return on Ad Spend (ROAS)**. For every dollar spent on advertising in a particular channel, how much sales revenue are we able to attribute back? While overall, an eCommerce business might be content with a ROAS of 5x, at the lower end of the funnel, we are striving for a minimum of 10-15x and aiming for 20-50x.

One of our specialist eCommerce retail clients was recently able to attribute $99 in sales revenue for every $1 spent - $66 was being delivered through their online store, whilst $33 was achieved in-store and reconciled back through data from their EPOS. Big numbers are possible at the lower stages of the funnel, but ONLY if the longer-term awareness and education activities are invested in further up the funnel.

CPA ("cost per acquisition" or "cost per action") is a useful secondary measure, as it indicates how much it costs to acquire each new conversion. Depending on how your back-end customer data is managed and integrated with your marketing analytics, you may be able to transcribe this into the cost to acquire a new customer, which is indeed a very powerful metric.

Finding and prioritizing channels, campaigns, creatives, and audiences that can yield customer segments with the highest lifetime profitability is the gold dust we should all be striving for.

Lower funnel is where we may want to invest most of our ad budget, but hopefully, at this stage, it is clear that effective long-term growth is fueled by a **well-balanced funnel**. Over time, we see anywhere from 30-70% of spend dedicated to lower funnel conversion campaigns.

Spend too much budget at the lower end of the funnel and acquisition costs will rise, conversion rates will decline, and the channels will become inefficient due to very high ad view frequencies. Spend too little, and you'll be missing very clear opportunities to nudge those undecided shoppers across the line.

A word of caution. It is **easy to over-invest at the lower end of the funnel** in activities that don't drive incremental gains. Consider Kyoto Sushi Bar who hires five teens to hand out coupons. After just a few days, one of the teens turns out to be a marketing whizz.

Customers keep turning up with coupon flyers from this one new recruit. The others can't figure it out and ask her, "What's your strategy?" "It's simple," she says. "I stand outside as people are queuing to go in." Most of us would conclude that she's not a marketing whizz, after all. It's easy and doesn't help with acquisition to give customers a coupon who are going to buy sushi anyway.

It's an easy trick for ad platforms to take credit for conversions that were going to take place anyway and therefore provide amazing ROI metrics for themselves. I tend to give the ad platforms the benefit of the doubt that they're not actually lying to us.

However, they try to control the game and will certainly encourage you to spend more where their metrics look good, even if they are not *causing* the conversion event.

In the next chapter, we'll dig deeper into how we can better understand the relative impact of different ad channels through the funnel. Then, in the final chapter, we'll see how we can use such information to optimize performance with either manual or automated tactics.

#5 Checklist

- → Connect the **product catalog** with ad channels to ensure shoppers are dynamically presented with relevant products in a timely manner.
- → Roll-out **dynamic creative ads** to allow the ad platforms to automatically test multiple variants of ad elements to drive higher engagement.
- → Highlight **offers, along with urgency and scarcity** messages to provide strong incentives for in-market customers to complete their purchase.
- → Develop capabilities to enable ad platforms to present personalized product messages to **in-market and unconverted** shoppers.
- → Flesh out **customer segments** based on recency, frequency, and monetary value of purchase, leveraging ad platforms to re-engage.
- → Launching an **influencer marketing** program can yield benefits further up the funnel, but with good tracking in place, can also deliver attributable sales.
- → Measure campaign performance with **Return on Ad Spend (ROAS)** metrics and aim to invest 30-70% of overall ad budget.

#6

MEASUREMENT & ATTRIBUTION

The goals of advertising will vary depending on the campaign objective aligned with our overall strategy of nudging audiences through the purchase funnel. When we're inspiring audiences with our unique story, we measure outcomes based on engagement with our video content. As we educate engaged audiences, we adjust our key metrics to the cost of delivering quality traffic to our web store. For our hot audiences, we are fully concentrated on return on ad spend (ROAS) and acquisition cost efficiencies.

Since every campaign is ultimately **supporting an overall revenue maximization or cost efficiency agenda**, we very often combine data from all campaigns to report on single umbrella metrics such as ROAS or CPA. This is all straightforward when advertising on a single platform, as the platform itself will consolidate data across campaigns.

However, when advertising across multiple ad platforms with potentially dozens of campaigns running at any one time, significant complexity can arise. The single most important question posed by digital advertisers charged with growing their business is: **where should I invest ad spend right now to deliver the best returns**? Without a clear understanding of which campaigns, regardless of ad channel, are delivering which impacts, we end up with significant waste and missed opportunity.

When advertising across multiple ad channels, it is impossible to achieve an accurate view of the true contribution of each channel. Let me repeat that so we are clear: **with cross-channel advertising today, it is impossible to achieve an accurate view of the true contribution of each ad campaign.** This might shock some people, because in an age when we believe everything is *measurable,* then surely it must be possible to join the dots with a degree of certainty?

It is not much to expect that we can easily assess the relative impact of ad campaigns across Facebook, Google, Amazon, or Microsoft!

Just listing the names of four of the biggest companies on the planet should provide the clue as to why I'm rather pessimistic about this problem being solved any time soon. It is simply not in any of the big players' interests to make this possible. Each ad platform is fighting to retain or acquire a greater share of your ad spend, so unless the data is likely to paint them in a better light, there is no commercial incentive to help you consolidate metrics. As soon as you do start to consolidate metrics, the transparency puts you back in control, which is not the game any of these platforms want to play.

We have entered an era of competition-fueled "siloization," when intransparency is the single biggest contributor to the phenomenal growth in advertising spend on a small number of platforms.

Each platform presents itself as a complete solution and, while they may privately acknowledge that their advertising clients will benefit from advertising across multiple channels, there is consistently very little collaboration between the platforms to facilitate any meaningful data interoperability.

If it is impossible to achieve a 100% accurate view of performance across ad channels, how can we come to a better appreciation of where value is being achieved? There are three types of solutions available to us as a result, with none being wholly adequate:

1. **Ad Platform Data -** We can rely on the data from the ad platforms themselves to understand what is taking place. Here, we end up with inflated contribution metrics since no individual channel takes into account the impact of other channels. Google Ads claims 100% of the conversions it can see, as does Facebook Ads, Microsoft Ads, Pinterest Ads and so on, without any deduplication.

2. **Analytics Tools -** Alternatively, we can plug in tracking such as Google Analytics, Adobe Analytics, or another third-party attribution tool and let them figure things out. In all cases where tracking is implemented on your site, you're missing all the data that the ad platforms don't share with third parties,

such as view-through conversion data or any audience-based data. Analytics will typically understate the impact of many ad channels but do this unequally since each platform performs in different ways through the funnel.

3. **eCommerce Platforms -** Your eCommerce engine (Shopify, WooCommerce, BigCommerce etc) will provide you with acquisition and sales referral data. In most cases these reports will show you only a single referring website that led to a specific session or sale. So, we only see the last thing a customer clicked on prior to purchase, which is likely to give us a very one-dimensional view of advertising impact.

Further discrepancies exist between the reports from eCommerce platforms, analytics tools, and ad channels; depending on how each records and defines specific different data points.[76] Unfortunately, there is no industry standard definition of how to record a session, visitor, or even a purchase!

So, we're pretty much stuck in a rut if we rely on any one of the ad platforms' data or the data coming from marketing analytics or eCommerce platform reports. The alternative (or the truth) lies somewhere in between.

Analytics tools combined with our eCommerce platform data can provide us with more accurate sales data *and* important signals about the relative impact of different advertising channels. Combined with the rich data from the ad platforms themselves, we can gain a more holistic view of the most important contributors to our growth. But this is a lot of work and requires ongoing detailed analysis.

Attribution

Given that there is no 100% accurate way to bridge the data gap between the big ad platforms, the industry has become somewhat obsessed with the topic of attribution. Attribution modeling in marketing refers to the analysis and understanding of the **relative contributions to sales** of the different touchpoints in a consumer purchase journey.

If a consumer buys an item on a website after clicking on a single ad, we can with some certainty credit that conversion entirely to that one ad. However, what if the path to purchase isn't as straightforward?

Maybe a customer viewed a display ad, then a Facebook ad a week later, before they visited the website from an organic search listing and then having received an email with a discount coupon, they finally completed a purchase.

How can we know which touchpoint or combination of touchpoints contributed most to that purchase? Marketing attribution is the attempt to answer this question. It is the practice of **evaluating the touchpoints a consumer encounters** on their path to purchase.

The goal of marketing attribution is to determine which channels and messages have the greatest impact on the decision to convert. A marketing attribution model will credit a specific touchpoint based on the contribution that touchpoint is assessed to have made to the conversion.

Attribution helps us determine **where to invest both money and time**, to grow our business efficiently. It helps us overcome preconceived notions about what might be making the biggest contribution and thus eliminates waste.

Companies who have not put adequate thought into their attribution model often default into a simple single-touch attribution model, such as "last touch." A last touch attribution model assigns 100% of the credit for a conversion to the very last thing someone did just before they purchased.

In the example above, a last touch model would assign 100% of the credit to the email with the discount code. All preceding activities are ignored and considered irrelevant, receiving zero credit. If we truly believed the results of such a model, we would make zero investment in anything that occurred prior to the email touchpoint.

Of course, this is **marketing nonsense** and yet single-touch attribution models dominate ROI analysis inside many organizations. Multi-touch attribution models, on the other hand, attempt to spread the credit for a conversion across the range of touchpoints engaged in by a user prior to purchase. We've seen time and again that the choice of attribution model can have a significant impact on understanding where value is being achieved.

Davina runs an eCommerce store shipping a specialist lifestyle product globally from her warehouse in Ireland. We recently worked with her to help her better understand the metrics available across the business. Like many eCommerce businesses, she relies heavily on Google Analytics, combined with her Shopify sales data, to help better understand where customers are coming from. She spends six figures on digital marketing over the course of a year and accounting for that spend is a high priority for her.

When looking at the default conversion reports in Google Analytics, Davina could see that paid media was being credited with 56% of website visits that ended in a sale. By default, Google Analytics reports on the last website a user came from immediately prior to purchase. When Davina switched to a more sophisticated multi-touch model, the volume of conversions attributed to paid media increased by over 25%. The real impact of advertising hadn't changed by switching the attribution model, but the capability to make smarter business decisions certainly had changed.

Let's align on our understanding of the most commonly used models across the industry in order to clarify when and if they may be useful to us.

"Last click" or "Last touch"

> "Last touch" is generally the default option chosen by advertisers, which isn't very surprising. It is very simple to understand and is also widely deployed and considered to be the "daddy" of attribution: the original of the species. In a nutshell, this methodology focuses on the last page or touchpoint before conversion, and it blindly assigns all credit to that touchpoint.

The problem with this model is that it does not account for any other engagements in the user journey that may have led to the conversion. Last touch can be appropriate in some cases, such as when you are only using a single channel. For commercial simplicity, many affiliate business models are based on last click attribution models. However, the path to purchase is getting more and more complex and customers are interacting with many different touchpoints before converting.

"Last non-direct click"

A twist on last click, "last non-direct click" is the default attribution model in Google Analytics.[77] Therefore, this is the attribution model that is used without question by more than half of all website owners.[78] Last non-direct click attribution assigns 100% of the credit for an event on your website to the last click that brought someone to your website, excluding "direct" visits. A direct visit is where someone types in your website URL in the address bar of their web browser.

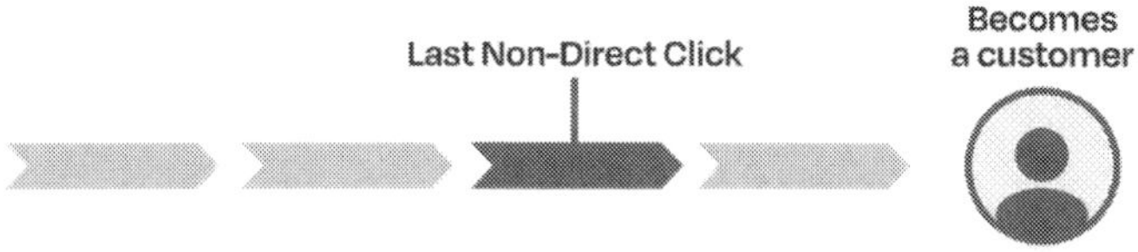

In this model, only referring clicks count. In the same way that direct visits are discounted, so too are impressions on your ads on third-party platforms. And because this is a single-touch model, all touchpoints prior to the last non-direct click are equally ignored.

"First click" or "First touch"

First touch attribution is another single-touch model which focuses exclusively on the initial engagement that the customer took on their journey and ignores any subsequent engagements they may have had prior to converting. This type of attribution model would suit a campaign where awareness was the main objective. The assumption is that if someone doesn't ever become aware of your product in the first place, they're never going to buy regardless of what else you might do.

The major drawback of this model is that it ignores other potentially important interactions after the first interaction. You put all that effort into inspiring a cold audience and then, assuming you act based on the data provided by this attribution model, shut down all other marketing activities. What a waste!

"Linear" or "Equal"

This model is arguably the most straightforward of the multi-touch attribution models. It identifies each touchpoint that led to a conversion and splits the credit for that conversion equally across all touchpoints. If there were, for example, 5 touchpoints leading to a single sale of $100, then each touchpoint would be assigned 20% of the credit for the conversion or $20 in attributed revenue.

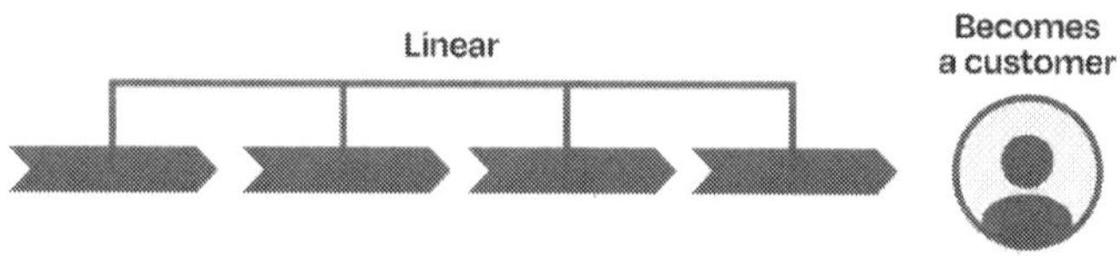

This model does not consider that different aspects of the consumer's journey can have a greater impact than others. While it is an improvement on single-touch models, it fails to account for the fact that different touchpoints may have had more or less of an impact on the customers decision to convert than others.

"Position based" or "U-shaped"

This model considers that the first and last touchpoints are probably the most impactful in the overall purchase journey. This model assigns the most credit to the first and final engagements. The remaining credit is assigned equally to any of the touchpoints that occurred after the first and before the last touchpoints. Typically, 40% credit is assigned each to the first engagement and the last touchpoint, with the remaining 20% distributed equally across the middle interactions.

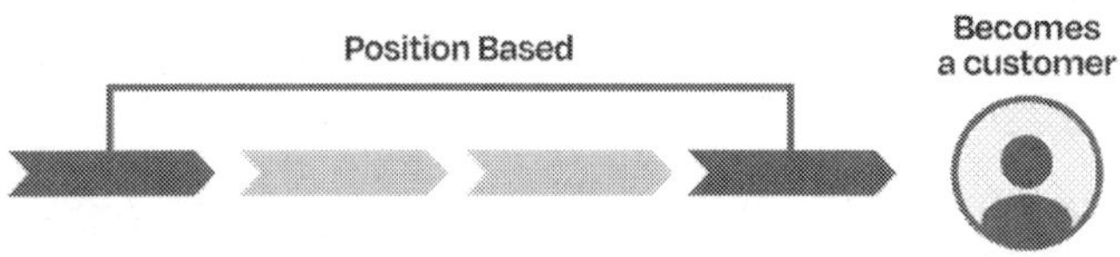

This u-shaped model has relevance, but it fails to accurately credit touchpoints in the middle of the journey which may have had a bigger impact on the conversion than the advertiser might expect. If you are selling a complex product that requires extensive consumer research, and which, say mid-funnel video may be invaluable to enabling the consumer to appreciate key features, it seems nonsensical to effectively down-weight this education activity in favor of a more recent ad click.

"Time-decay"

"Time decay/delay" is another multi-touch attribution model. It credits all touchpoints on a user journey, but weighs credit more heavily to touchpoints that occurred closer to the time of conversion than those further back in time. In some variants there is a half-life of 7 days which means that an interaction that took place a week prior to the conversion event will receive half the credit received by an interaction on the day of conversion. These models consider recency of engagement as the most important factor across touchpoints.

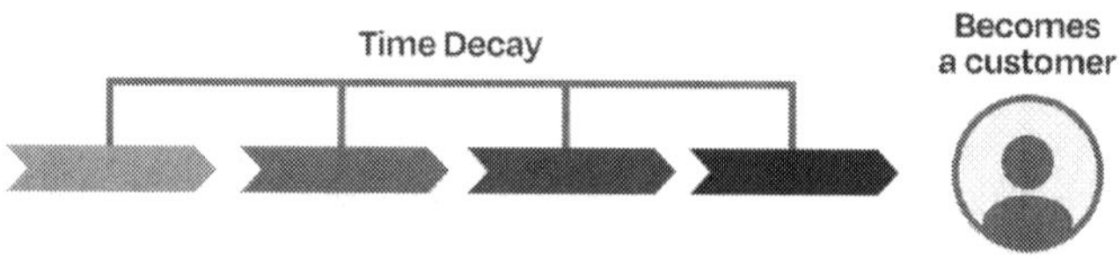

Some marketers use this model for high intensity short burst campaigns, perhaps over a couple of days. Others use it when the path-to-purchase can take several months. Once again, this model doesn't take into consideration any qualitative impacts of different campaign components, such as the time spent watching a detailed product video, which may have occurred very early in the purchase cycle.

"Data-driven" or "Algorithmic"

Data-driven attribution is another multi-touch type model, dynamically using actual historical performance data, as opposed to the rigid rules used by all of the other models. Such models are typically more mathematically complex, using either predefined algorithms or machine learning or a combination of both. These models will usually evolve over time, learning based on real-world data from live campaigns.

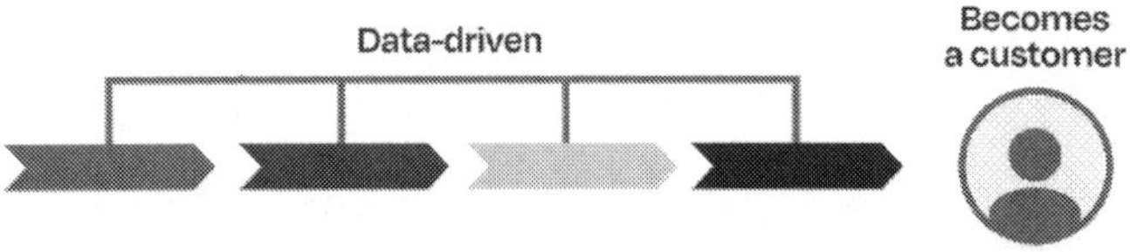

Perhaps the most prevalent data-driven model, used within the Google suite of products, is based on game theory algorithms devised by U.S. mathematical economist and Nobel Laureate Lloyd Shapley.[79] The Shapley game theory approach considers how to fairly assign credit to individual "players" based on their assessed contribution to the overall team goal of winning a game. Applied to marketing attribution, it attempts to fairly model how much each marketing touchpoint (player) working in a coalition with other touchpoints, contributes to the marketer's goal of driving conversions.

When used in marketing attribution, the Shapley algorithm calculates the **conditional probability of each touchpoint having impacted** on conversion. It compares the conversion probability of consumers exposed to multiple touchpoints to the probability of conversion when one of those touchpoints does not occur in the path. It also takes into consideration the sequence of events.

The major benefit of data-driven attribution modelling is

that the outcomes adapt based on your unique set of circumstances. Rigid rules are abandoned for probabilistic modelling which is anchored on your own customers' behaviors over time. Note that it is used very often using only click-based data points and, therefore, can provide little credit to activities further up the funnel.

Attribution is like **waking up with a hangover**. Do you (like me) give 100% of the blame to the tequila shot you had at the end of a long night? If we had a scientist on hand to study our behavior through the previous evening, I'm sure they would develop a more statistically valid explanation based on empirical evidence.

Why is it then, that in the professional field of marketing, we have been so tolerant with maintaining the "default" attribution models that have been handed down to us by vested interests? Are we all still drunk?

Marketing Mix Modelling

Another approach to identifying the impact of marketing across channels is Marketing Mix Modelling (MMM). MMM is a measurement technique, used traditionally across non-digital channels (TV, print), to attribute incremental sales to marketing and non-marketing activities. It uses historical data and various algorithms to draw conclusions about the impacts of marketing spend over time on sales performance.[80]

The statistical methods underlying MMM work on assumptions over very long periods of time with stable inputs. Frankly, time and again, **digital channels don't seem**

to fare well in these studies. It is no wonder, therefore, that you won't have to dig too hard to see criticisms from the big digital players on the use of these types of models.

"Most of the time, MMM isn't set up to provide actionable insights when it comes to digital," says Google.[81] "Modern platforms such as Facebook's family of apps and services have dynamic, nuanced advertising possibilities and are constantly evolving to keep up with shifts in consumer behavior. This makes assessing their true influence far more difficult compared with established channels such as print and television." says Facebook.[82]

The lesson here is that if you are going to invest in MMM in order to drive optimization activities, ensure that you consider the rapidly changing and evolving dynamics of digital marketing. If interested, dig into the details of the typical offering from one of the big consulting houses. Even these big data nerds who will run the most sophisticated mathematical models will ultimately (and unsurprisingly) conclude; "there isn't a straightforwardly linear relationship between sales and marketing channels."[83]

Universal Marketing Metrics

The fundamental lack of data interoperability between the ad channels, analytics tools and eCommerce platforms means that a single source of truth is not possible. Even the most sophisticated data-driven attribution models are only able to work with the data available to them and in today's completely siloized advertising world, there is a lot of data missing. Marketing-mix modelling can feel like boiling the ocean.

Given all of this complexity, we've started to see a movement towards a more universal approach to measurement and attribution across channels. A "universal metrics" approach begins with the assumption that while no source of data is 100% reliable, all sources provide **important and useful performance signals** which shouldn't be ignored.

So, rather than treat data from any one source as gospel, this approach **consolidates, normalizes and analyzes** the data patterns and trends across all sources to make **better predictions about which channels will accelerate future growth**.

For universal metrics, you will **consolidate data from as many relevant sources** as possible. As an eCommerce advertiser, you will be interested in the data available from within the ad platforms, such as Google Ads, Facebook Ads, Pinterest Ads, Microsoft Ads, and even Amazon Ads. However, you'll understand that in all cases the self-attributed conversions from an ad campaign are overstated, as none fully considers the role of other paid and organic marketing activities.

You will also be interested in the data available from your **web analytics** solution, such as those provided by Google, Adobe, and many other third parties. Within these tools you may be able to adjust attribution models to provide a more holistic view of customers' paths to purchase. However, you'll always be missing some very critical proprietary data not exposed by the ad platforms to third parties.

And finally, you'll be interested in the data from your **eCommerce engine**. The data here provides a much fuller understanding of customer lifetime values and longer-term customer behaviors. Here, you'll be missing the complete picture of your advertising activities and the paths-to-purchase your customers took prior to that last click from an email or brand keyword search.

No individual data source today can offer you a full and accurate picture of your cross-channel marketing performance. However, **each data source provides important performance *signals***, which, when combined, are extremely powerful in shaping business decisions for growth.

In this approach, firstly consolidate data from the different sources. The data is then normalized to ensure we are comparing apples with apples. In Optily, our algorithms then **calculate a weighting for each data point based on the impact** on past and predicted future performance.

The ad channel claims a ROAS of 20x, but the analytics platform's data suggests a ROAS of 4x for that ad channel. By understanding that the truth is somewhere in the middle, and based on predictive modelling, using these data signals, we can get much closer to the real current contribution of each channel and future potential impact of various investment adjustments.

When used to optimize budget strategies, universal marketing metrics have enabled our own clients to achieve improvements of at least 30-70% in advertising ROI over a relatively short period and sustained 3-4x growth in the longer term. By simply changing **how we measure ad impact** across channels, we can radically improve performance almost overnight.

Without a solid multi-touchpoint measurement and attribution strategy, it is very difficult to consistently achieve ever-improving ROI results and grow your business. Reliable metrics allow you to take more control of the consumer journey and then shape it in accordance with your needs and desired outcomes.

Implementing a universal metrics strategy allows for greater efficiency, by allocating resources to channels that are objectively performing the best. With comprehensive data and the tools to unlock it, multi-channel marketing can be more accurate and agile, perfectly suited to today's world of increasingly complex customer journeys.

Measurement and attribution are hard. It is no wonder that it remains at the very top of the list of topics that marketers lose sleep over.[84] Without reliable data, strategy has no basis.

#6 Checklist

- → Ensure **reporting capabilities** are in place across ad channels, analytics tools, and eCommerce or internal systems.
- → Determine which **attribution model** to rely on and develop reporting solutions that reliably report on marketing events using this model.
- → Identify if **marketing mix modelling** is an appropriate investment to provide insights into long-term marketing impacts.
- → Consider leveraging **universal marketing metrics** approach to consolidate, normalize, and analyze performance across ad channels.
- → Commence **adjusting budgets** based on unified metrics across the funnel to determine potential impacts on ROI.

#7

OPTIMIZATION FOR GROWTH

Adam is an eCommerce marketer working for an online store specializing in cleaning products for truck owners. Adam was scaling up rapidly using Facebook and Instagram ads. He was able to achieve significant efficiencies in ad spend by reviewing and adjusting campaign budgets up to three times per day. The business was flying, but the constant attention required to manage advertising spend in just one ad platform left him with very little time for other parts of his job.

Adam was eager to get started with Google and Microsoft ads, as he perceived that his product line would be competitive in the search environment. Like many eCommerce marketers, Adam **wants to stay in control** of digital advertising, however, with limited time in the day, Adam was stuck. He simply didn't have time to do everything.

Adam and I first started talking at the point where he was searching for workflow automation solutions that would allow him to streamline the almost hourly tasks of analyzing and adjusting ad campaigns for growth.

For someone like Adam, there are several options available. While the ad platforms themselves do provide optimization capabilities, very often they don't provide the levels of control that many of us require.

In addition, when you **add multiple channels** to your marketing mix, the optimization task quickly becomes impossible for any one person. With a whole range of controls at our fingertips, where should we invest our time and efforts to achieve the highest returns?

There are a number of "manual" optimization tasks that you can focus on to ensure your campaigns are set up for success. Get these right up-front and you can spend less time fixing things later. Happily, the ad platforms are also increasingly providing "automated" optimization controls which enable you to reduce the volume of analysis, decision-making and tinkering tasks. These come with some pitfalls, as we'll see shortly.

Often, when advertising across multiple ad channels, you need to step outside the individual ad channels and apply third-party solutions to provide prioritized actionable insights to help you grow more efficiently. Let's look at these options in turn.

Manual Campaign Optimization

You've created your ad campaigns and are not getting the

results you expected. What are the key things you can do to improve your outcomes? Use this checklist to ensure you are set up for success from the outset.

- **Campaign Objectives -** Ensure that the campaign objectives you have set within the campaign are aligned with your business goals. For example, if you are really measuring ROAS but the campaign is set up with a conversion objective for landing page views, you've got a problem.

- **Pixel / Server-to-server / Offline Conversion Tracking -** Ad platforms optimize based on the data they have available to them. Ensure the data feeding back from your website or offline events is flowing seamlessly. Get to grips with all the privacy and data balances for your business. Ensure the various events (page views, button clicks) are firing correctly. Without these signals the ad platforms are shooting blind.

- **Audience Targeting -** If your audience is not aligned with your product offering or objectives, you may spend huge amounts on people who have no interest in your services. Review campaign performance for different audience segments - if possible, structure your campaigns so that you can easily understand which audiences deliver higher returns.

- **Audience Exclusions -** Exclude audiences that you

don't want to target. Recent purchasers for a product that people don't by frequently repeat buy is the most obvious example. How often have you seen an ad from a site for the product you bought from them a week ago?

- **Creative Variants -** We have rarely had a problem of too much creative. Most platforms and third-party optimization solutions enable you to multi-variant test creative and audience combinations. The more creative variants you can make available, the better chance you have of finding gold.

- **Creative Refresh -** While you are continuously hunting for free audiences, it is very often the case that refreshing your creatives can kick-start tired campaigns. Don't make changes for the sake of it, but if nothing else is working, consider updating your messages and visuals.

- **Frequency Overload -** As soon as you overload a specific audience, there's a high chance that your overall performance will start to decline. Frequency is how often a specific creative has been seen by the audience in a specific campaign. Hitting frequencies of 5 or 6 typically indicates that your audience is too small or your need to refresh your creative.

- **Negative Keywords -** Negative keywords let you filter out clicks that are less valuable to you or that are false positives - people searching for something with a similar name to your brand or product, but in a completely different category.

- **Adding Keywords -** Ad platforms will typically suggest new keywords which can help you increase your reach. These suggestions are based on a mix of your existing campaigns' ads, landing pages, and keywords. You will also be able to see bid suggestions and an estimated performance impact of those new keywords.

- **Budget Reallocation -** By reviewing campaign performance, you will quickly see which campaigns are delivering the best returns right now. Remember, the ad platforms are sophisticated auctions whereby you are bidding to have your message seen by a desired audience. Moving the budget to the part of the auction that is delivering for you today is a great way to improve your ability to scale.

Automated Campaign Optimization

In addition to the range of manual interventions, the ad platforms offer an ever-increasing range of options for you to automate common tasks. This allows smaller advertisers to leverage advanced machine-learning to drive better performance. A word of caution here, as simply switching on automation will not always lead to the outcomes you might expect.

- **Dynamic Ads -** As we've seen earlier, the platforms understand their own audiences' behavior better than anyone. Leverage dynamic creative ads and dynamic catalog ads to maximize the chances that the right message will hit the right customer at the right time. Each platform provides a nuanced offering, and these formats are definitely worth including in your overall mix.

- **Smart Display Ads (Google)** – Google's "Display Network" enables you to have your banner ads appear on millions of publisher websites across the globe. Smart Display Ads is an approach that automates bidding for display ads based on a target CPA that you set. Automated targeting within this campaign-types accelerates focus on audiences most likely to convert. Plus, ads are dynamically created from various elements uploaded to the ad platform.

- **Smart Shopping Ads (Google) -** Google's combination of your product catalog and machine learning bidding is rather powerful and is where many store owners often start. You can simply connect your Shopify, WooCommerce, or Big Commerce store with Google and you're off. The downside with these ads is that Google provides extremely limited data which you might want to use to inform other campaign strategies.

- **Automated Bidding -** Automated bidding takes the

heavy lifting out of setting bids for ads. You set parameters in your campaign and the platform decides what bids to place. Google provides six different automated bidding strategies that align with your different business objectives. Target CPA, for example, automatically sets Search or Display bids to help get as many conversions as possible at the target cost-per-action (CPA).

- **Campaign Budget Optimization (Facebook & Instagram) -** Campaign Budget Optimization from Facebook Ads automatically moves budget from ad sets with higher cost per action (CPA) to ad sets with lower CPA, thus ensuring your spend is most efficient. This is a great tool for already established campaigns to maximize performance. Early on, we find that specific ad sets can be either over or under-funded based on the peculiarities of the Facebook algorithms, so tread cautiously.

- **Automatic Placements -** You may have some specific ideas about where you'd like your ads to be seen. When you select "automatic placements" within ad platforms you enable their algorithms to deliver your ads dynamically, based on where they'll get the best performance. You may still want to exclude some placements, so make sure you know where you don't want your ads to appear and include those settings.

- **Automated Rules -** Automation rules and alerts allow you to set specific parameters for when you want something to occur. For example, you want to run a specific campaign within a certain timeframe, you can set a rule that dictates when the campaign automatically goes live and is paused again.

- **Daily vs Lifetime Budget -** You often have a choice as to whether you set a daily or lifetime budget for your campaign. Daily gives you greater control on a day-to-day basis on how much is spent. Lifetime budget controls the total spend of a campaign but gives more flexibility to the ad platforms to adjust the pacing over time, based on performance.

When you choose automated optimization settings you will become more aware of the **"learning" phase**. Before automated tasks kick in, each platform will have different criteria for the volume of data its algorithms need to make decisions. You should expect to wait 2-3 days or when around 50 conversion events have taken place before automated optimization fully kicks in.

Cross-channel Optimization

While many of us start with a single ad platform, typically Facebook Ads or Google Ads, there comes a point for most of us where we need to deploy our messaging consistently across multiple platforms.

The main drivers for multi-channel advertising are a combination of:

- **Maximizing reach** - each platform provides different opportunities to reach different audiences and often these audiences are mutually exclusive. For example, a Bing or Yahoo! search user might prefer to use these platforms and rarely uses Google search.

- **Visibility across the funnel** - different types of platforms play different roles through the funnel. For example, social is great for inspiring interest amongst broad audiences, while search is great for closing out shoppers with high purchase intent.

- **Efficiency across the funnel** – each placement comes with its strengths at different stages in the purchase journey. Committing to a single ad platform will reduce your capability to drive cost efficiencies as you seek to engage with shoppers in external environments.

Costs and effort **can quickly escalate** when you add a second or third ad platform into your mix. In addition to the problem of measurement and attribution we discussed earlier, there's the constant challenge of identifying and acting on opportunities to maximize returns or reduce waste.

How do you approach this? Do you hire more people with the necessary skills and expertise across different platforms? Do you engage a media-buying agency and leverage their range of skills and experience? Do you leverage a rules-based or intelligent software solution to automate changes?

Whichever approach you take, watch out for the natural tendency towards siloization. Very often we see that the personnel skilled in paid social are different to those skilled in paid search. Power users of different ad platforms tend to be specialists and rarely overlap. If you find the unicorns who can do both effectively, then great! Hire them!

In agencies, the gap in skills is often even wider than with an in-house team. The paid social team in an agency is often *competing* with the paid search team internally for relevance and share of advertising wallet. This may seem bizarre to advertisers, however, within big media agencies, the main internal metric for success is how much spend you can extract from your clients. This usually leads to the wrong incentives for everyone involved.

When I first met Keith and Ciaran, co-founders of Optily, I was impressed with their **mission to break down the internal silos** that often exist both in agencies and in-house marketing teams. I jumped on board with the guys because I believed their approach of bringing an independent technology-driven solution to smash through the walls was unique and compelling.

Originally, Optily had created a solution that enabled large-scale ad agencies to automatically adjust bid and budget strategies in real time across multiple channels, by creating a unique data bridge between Facebook Ads Manager and Google's Agency Platform. This approach relies on performance signals from data-driven attribution models in

Google's Campaign Manager (agency toolkit) to determine the optimal settings for campaigns in Facebook, Instagram, Google, YouTube, and the Google DV360 programmatic display platform.

Customers were seeing dramatic results very quickly - achieving up to 3x more conversions with the same ad spend in a very short space of time. Why did this work? Facebook's algorithms, for example, simply can't see which other touchpoints from different channels a user engages with on their path to purchase, and therefore goes all-in on any specific ad or audience segment that it can attribute a sale to.

A cross-channel attribution model can see which ads and audiences in Facebook are having the highest impact on conversions. Optily's algorithms can prioritize those high impact ads specifically; automatically adjusting bids and budgets to deliver a higher return. This solution is now used by many of the biggest advertisers and ad agencies globally.

Google's Campaign Manager is a powerful enterprise solution that comes with significant cost and complexity. However, scaling online businesses today typically rely on data from a mix of their ad platforms, analytics tools, and eCommerce platforms to inform optimization decisions.

As a result, the second generation of the Optily cross-channel optimization tool enables in-house and performance agency teams to automatically adjust ad campaigns across multiple channels, based on unified marketing metrics across the funnel. Digital marketers can easily consolidate and normalize data from disparate reporting solutions and access insights on opportunities to improve performance.

With an automation solution such as Optily, a cross-channel marketer can, for example, move budget from one campaign in Google to a campaign in Facebook because that campaign is performing much better right now. Insights can be actioned in real time when automation is enabled. This means that in-house teams can reduce time spent ensuring that budgets and other campaign settings are continually set to deliver the highest returns from the constantly changing ad auction.

Early customers have described the impact of this solution as giving them back both time and control: two desperately needed commodities for today's modern marketer. Adam, our truck washing supplies friend, was able to reduce his daily engagement with ad campaigns to a matter of minutes from several hours. In addition, within the first 14 days his **ROAS increased by 169%**, across a mix of Facebook and Google lower funnel campaigns. Nice start!

#7 Checklist

→ Upon **launching campaigns,** ensure objectives are appropriate, event tracking is in place, audiences are relevant, and creative variants exist.

→ As **campaigns progress**, monitor creative refresh, frequency overload, keyword appropriateness, and budget allocations.

→ Deploy **automated optimizations,** such as dynamic ads, "smart" campaigns, automated budget allocations, and placements.

→ Be aware of the **limitations of automation** and the necessity for all algorithmic based automations to complete their "learning phases."

→ Develop a **cross-channel strategy** that ensures you are maximizing reach, improving visibility, and efficiency across the funnel.

→ Deploy **automated cross-channel optimization** solutions (such as Optily) to ensure waste is reduced and growth opportunities are seized.

CONCLUSION

As I write these last few sentences, the world of digital advertising is becoming more diversified and yet the giants are consolidating their positions further. There are probably no more than seven or eight ad companies that are relevant to digital marketers in the western world, however, two of these own the game. No matter how big you are, you are a minnow when it comes to the power of these big platforms. I've seen a national retailer spending millions of dollars with one of these big platforms fail spectacularly in unlocking any concessions. So how can any of us win?

The most sophisticated digital marketer will consider engaging with the ad platforms owned by one or more of these companies: Google, Facebook, Microsoft, Amazon, Twitter, Snap, or Pinterest. In 2020, the combined global advertising revenue generated by these companies grew by 15% to a whopping $278 billion.[85] However, just two companies, Google and Facebook accounted for nearly 83% of that advertising spend.

So, while the Internet has democratized access to national and international markets for many small and mid-sized businesses, that access is controlled by a couple of dictators. These two Goliaths between them control the game and continually seek to increase their control.

Google is great at what it does in search, but it buys DoubleClick and YouTube to control even more categories. Facebook is an awesome social platform, and it buys Instagram and WhatsApp to control more of that game. We love the capabilities these platforms provide us to find and communicate with customers, but we want to take back control and reduce the waste.

One thing we can do is ensure that we diversify our investment. The biggest growth in advertising revenue in 2020 was experienced by Amazon (+53% YoY) and Pinterest (+48% YoY) and Snapchat (+46% YoY). So, while the big guys continue to dominate and cannot be ignored, there are some new and interesting platforms available to us at a scale not seen before.

Advertisers are investing more and more into these new platforms, which are creating innovative ways for us to engage more consumers. Snapchat, for example, has brought the world of AR onto everyone's smartphone, enabling shoppers to explore our products in the context of their own real-world environment.

As advertisers, **we are agnostic** to the channel we use, conscious only of the capabilities offered by each to deliver efficient and effective advertising strategies. We have become multi-channel marketers in a very short period, simply because our customers are to be found in a myriad of different places. TikTok, for example, claims that 40% of its users are not on Facebook's platform at all.

My advice to Bob, who inspired this book, is to take a step back from the disappointing early results in Google. Bob wants to fuel the growth of his nascent eCommerce business. The role of advertising is to support his owned and operated eCommerce marketing activities. Pouring gas on a damp fire will result in some initial excitement but will likely end in frustration. We've seen that there are some logical steps that Bob can take to ensure his growth accelerates efficiently when adding the fuel of paid advertising.

Ensuring these **five fundamental eCommerce pillars** are in place from the outset will help to accelerate the impact of paid media:

1. **Differentiation**
   How is my offering better than the rest?
2. **Discoverability**
   How easy is it for potential customers to find us?
3. **Conversion Rate Optimization**
   How effective is our website at converting?
4. **Customer Relationship Management**
   Are we building direct customer relationships?
5. **Data Layer**
   Can we reliably leverage customer data?

While Bob might be skeptical about using 100-year-old marketing strategies, the concept of leveraging advertising to **nurture buyers through their purchase journey** is still highly relevant.

Whether a customer makes an instantaneous decision to

purchase or spends several months researching options prior to purchase, behavioral scientists have identified three key stages in the buying decision:

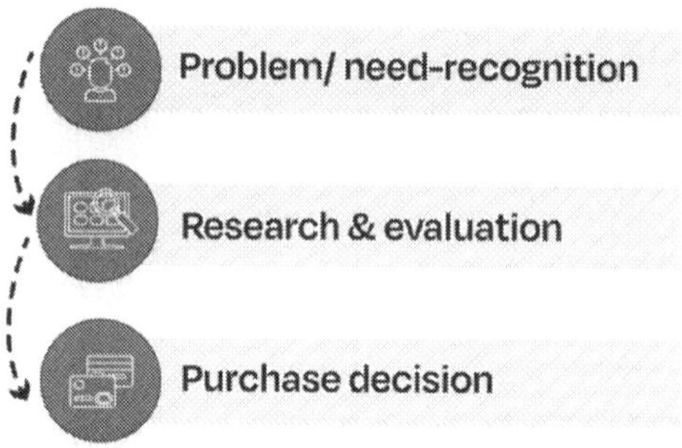

1. Firstly, consumers need to actively recognize a **problem** to solve, a **need** to fulfill or a **desire** to satisfy.

2. This is followed by consumers undertaking **research** into and **evaluation** of different potential solutions and offerings.

3. The third and ultimate **purchase decision** stage is found to be affected by cognitive biases plus input and feedback from others.

Our advertising strategy sets out to support buyers at each stage of the buying decision.

We seek to **inspire** those audiences who may be in-market for our solution but are unaware of our offering or even that there are solutions to the problem they experience.

↓

We want to **educate** shoppers who are aware of our offering but are still researching and evaluating options.

↓

And, of course, we need to **convince** shoppers with high purchase intent, helping them overcome purchase objections and nudging them to make that final purchase decision in our favor.

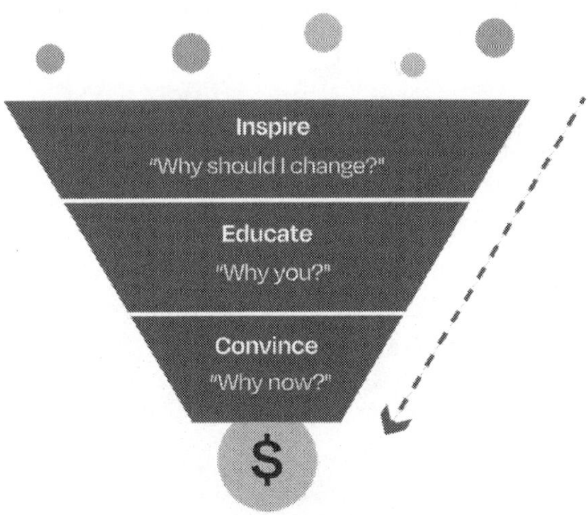

We might be tempted to focus all our attention on those lower funnel shoppers, however, for maximum efficiency and long-term growth, we have learned to **spread our attention and investments** across the funnel.

At our disposal to achieve our goals, is a mix of dynamics and capabilities across multiple advertising channels. At each stage of the funnel, we've seen how **creative** is the single biggest contributor to sales by any specific advertising element. From storytelling at the top of the funnel to clever integration of our product inventory with the ad platforms at the lower end of the funnel, there are now so many options available for us to inspire, educate, and convince digital shoppers.

Managing **audience-building** across channels is a significant lever for efficient funnel management. Going too broad too early, leads to wastage. Going too narrow, can quickly lead to lost opportunity and high costs. Choosing the right context and leveraging the peculiar dynamics of each ad channel can be highly impactful on our overall results.

Choosing the right **metrics** throughout our funnel is critical for making the right decisions. Upper-funnel engagement as we measure the impact of our brand storytelling is a quantum of difference to lower funnel ROAS and conversion efficiency. As marketers we find ourselves increasing balancing spend across the funnel to deliver the highest return possible from available budgets.

In the age of multi-channel digital advertising, marketers continue to struggle with clearly identifying where to invest ad spend right in a timely manner to deliver the best returns. Unfortunately, with cross-channel advertising today, it is **impossible to achieve an accurate view of the true**

contribution of each distinct advertising activity. However, we can leverage data from across ad channels, analytics tools, and eCommerce platforms to help us achieve a clearer view on which aspects of our advertising mix are delivering the highest contribution. A **universal marketing metrics** approach consolidates and normalizes data from across multiple sources, providing coherent insights and predictions for growth opportunities.

As we seek to **optimize our advertising** to help us accelerate our eCommerce growth, there are many controls at our fingertips. The ad platforms provide optimization capabilities which we can adjust either manually or using automation native to the platforms.

As we **combine multiple ad channels** in our marketing mix, the optimization task quickly becomes extremely challenging. Thankfully, there are third-party tools which enable us to untangle attribution and leverage unified data in automated ways to help us better achieve our outcomes.

Building an eCommerce store is a little like assembling your own racing kart from a kit. You are connecting a lot of moving parts to help you compete effectively on the racetrack. When it works well, you can accelerate and stay ahead of your competitors. However, when fundamental elements, such as your axles, are misaligned, you might be moving forward but are not making great progress.

So, we fix the alignment problem and then add more fuel, to go faster and start to win. Add fuel *before* you fix the alignment and you're likely to end up on your head.

Get all the moving parts of your eCommerce business aligned then add the fuel of digital advertising. Now you can sit back and watch your growth accelerate like never before.

Tell us what you think

If you found this book useful, please feel free to leave an honest review on Amazon. Search: "**Accelerate eCommerce Growth**".

Thanks!

ABOUT THE AUTHOR

Brendan J. Hughes has been "doing" eCommerce and digital marketing since 1997. His first commercial project was building the public website for Trinity College, Dublin, where he was a postgraduate student in computer science. Since then, he has worked inside numerous consumer brands delivering successful eCommerce transformations.

For much of his career he has been responsible for devising eCommerce and digital marketing strategies to help businesses accelerate their growth. In each of those roles, Brendan was confronted with the perennial challenge of buying media across multiple platforms and how to get the best returns from across the big walled gardens of Facebook and Google.

Brendan was Chief Digital Officer at Independent News & Media (INM plc), where he was responsible for the development of paid digital media offerings of the newspaper group. During this time, "on the other side of the fence" as he describes it himself, he saw how challenged the ad industry was. Writing in the Irish Marketing Journal in July 2017, he called on the industry to explain how up to "60% of advertising spend disappears into a black hole." Hughes was a board member of IAB (Interactive Advertising Bureau) at that time and committed himself to developing synergies between publishers to counteract the imbalances in the media landscape.

Over time, Brendan got to know the co-founders of an ad-tech start-up called Optily. The co-founders include Keith O'Reilly and Irish rugby legend Ciaran FitzGerald, who dedicated his post-rugby career to developing effective advertising solutions for retailers. Optily's mission is to level the playing field for small and medium-sized businesses advertising on the big ad platforms, such as Facebook and Google. Brendan joined Optily as CEO, realizing that the self-service solution developed by the team was a game-changer for eCommerce marketers.

Brendan travels between Optily's Austin office and Dublin, where he lives with his wife Anne and their three children. When he's not talking or writing about eCommerce and advertising, you'll find him sailing a Laser dinghy in Dublin Bay.

REFERENCES

[1] https://hbr.org/2016/05/your-whole-company-needs-to-be-distinctive-not-just-your-product

[2] https://www.optily.com/digital-marketing-tactics/developing-user-personas/

[3] https://cxl.com/guides/bounce-rate/benchmarks/

[4] https://www.invespcro.com/blog/the-average-website-conversion-rate-by-industry/

[5] https://neilpatel.com/blog/10-advanced-seo-techniques-thatll-double-your-search-traffic/

[6] https://www.optily.com/ecommerce/the-complete-guide-to-ecommerce-seo/

[7] https://www.searchenginejournal.com/seo-101/meet-search-engines/

[8] https://www.mdgadvertising.com/marketing-insights/infographics/the-shift-to-native-advertising-in-marketing-infographic/

[9] https://www.businessinsider.com/mobile-commerce-shopping-trends-stats?r=US&IR=T

[10] https://www.pingdom.com/blog/page-load-time-really-affect-bounce-rate/

[11] https://developers.google.com/speed/pagespeed/insights/?url=amazon.com&tab=mobile

[12] https://sleeknote.com/blog/e-commerce-conversion-rate-optimization

[13] https://learn.g2.com/customer-reviews-statistics

[14] https://neilpatel.com/blog/best-exit-overlay-strategies/

[15] https://www.bigcommerce.com/blog/chatbots/#chatbots-now-and-in-our-future

[16] https://info.monetate.com/rs/092-TQN-434/images/Monetate_EQ4_2015_A_Tale_of_Two_Visitors-web.pdf

[17] https://www.marketingprofs.com/charts/2016/30705/triggered-email-benchmarks-for-e-commerce-brands

[18] https://www.bluecore.com/resources/2020-retail-email-benchmark-report/

[19] https://econsultancy.com/e-commerce-stats-the-importance-of-returning-customers/

[20] https://www.optily.com/digital-marketing-tactics/what-happens-to-our-ads-when-the-cookies-go-away/

[21] https://www.optily.com/ad-platforms/google-scraps-third-party-cookies-in-chrome/

[22] https://blog.google/products/ads-commerce/2021-01-privacy-sandbox/

[23] https://www.optily.com/ecommerce/mastering-the-facebook-conversions-api-with-shopify/

[24] https://en.wikipedia.org/wiki/AIDA_(marketing)

[25] https://www.thinkwithgoogle.com/feature/search-intent-marketing-funnel/#/

[26] https://www.creditcards.com/credit-card-news/online-shopping-survey/

[27] https://www.searchenginejournal.com/understand-marketing-funnel/312569/

[28] https://www.thinkwithgoogle.com/consumer-insights/consumer-journey/navigating-purchase-behavior-and-decision-making/

[29] https://effworks.co.uk/wp-content/uploads/2017/10/MEDIA_IN_FOCUS_FINAL_PDF_909.pdf

[30] https://www.effworks.co.uk/ten-best-charts-binet-field/

[31] https://www.cbinsights.com/research/subscription-e-commerce-market-map-company-list/

[32] https://www.nielsen.com/us/en/insights/article/2017/when-it-comes-to-advertising-effectiveness-what-is-key/

[33] https://www.thinkwithgoogle.com/intl/en-gb/marketing-strategies/video/branding-video-advertising/

[34] http://youtube.com/watch?v=vT7yBn1KYl4

[35] https://www.youtube.com/watch?v=zo7DO3QpHI8

[36] https://www.youtube.com/watch?v=cF92NB4Pkl4

[37] https://www.chamber.media/see-videos/

[38] http://youtube.com/watch?v=f83AYIJiQUw

[39] http://youtube.com/watch?v=dkNIjo63Xsk

[40] https://www.facebook.com/business/news/5-graphs-to-change-the-way-you-understand-mobile-video-and-tv

[41] https://digiday.com/media/silent-world-facebook-video/

[42] https://www.wochit.com/blog/social-video-performance-index-2017/

[43] https://www.wochit.com/blog/new-report-shows-makes-viral-video/

[44] https://www.thinkwithgoogle.com/marketing-strategies/video/youtube-bumper-ads-best-practices-video-editing/

[45] https://www.thinkwithgoogle.com/consumer-insights/consumer-trends/consumer-intent-video-data/

[46] https://www.facebook.com/business/success/jubly-umph

[47] https://searchengineland.com/youtube-how-to-searches-up-70-yoy-with-over-100m-hours-of-how-to-videos-watched-in-2015-220773

[48] https://www.youtube.com/watch?v=ZUG9qYTJMsI

[49] http://youtube.com/intl/en-GB/ads/success-story/tulanes-closet/

[50] https://www.youtube.com/watch?v=vB-ARTu4HfM

[51] https://www.facebook.com/carouselformat/

[52] https://instapage.com/blog/google-gallery-ads

[53] https://www.facebook.com/business/ads/collection-ad-format

[54] https://forbusiness.snapchat.com/advertising/ad-formats/collection-ads

[55] https://blog.google/products/ads/new-ways-to-drive-action/

[56] https://cdn.shopify.com/static/future-of-commerce/Shopify%20Future%20of%20Commerce%202021.pdf

[57] https://www.facebook.com/business/ads/instant-experiences-ad-destination

[58] https://www.get-plop.com/case-studies/swyft

[59] https://forbusiness.snapchat.com/inspiration/clearly-used-snapchats-to-drive-a-purchase-lift-with-virtual-try-on

[60] https://forbusiness.snapchat.com/inspiration/ponds-utilized-multi-format-strategy-to-drive-purchase-intent-and-awareness-in-mexico

[61] https://forbusiness.snapchat.com/inspiration/snapchat-drives-40-higher-roi-for-nisnass

[62] https://www.facebook.com/business/success/2-we-make-up

[63] https://neilpatel.com/blog/long-tail-keywords-seo/

[64] https://www.thinkwithgoogle.com/consumer-insights/consumer-journey/search-video-purchase-journey/

[65] https://baymard.com/lists/cart-abandonment-rate

[66] https://www.facebook.com/business/success/espadrij-loriginale

[67] https://www.facebook.com/business/success/jd-williams

[68] https://ads.google.com/intl/en_uk/home/success-stories/topps-tiles/

[69] https://www.velocidi.com/blog/6-9x-roas-buyer-intent-predictions/

[70] https://en.wikipedia.org/wiki/Don%27t_be_evil

[71] https://support.google.com/adspolicy/answer/6118#keywords

[72] https://www.factor-a.de/wp-content/uploads/2019/02/Sponsored_Advertising_Whitepaper-EN-Web.pdf

[73] https://www.optily.com/content/does-my-business-need-influencers/

[74] https://blog.twitter.com/en_us/a/2016/new-research-the-value-of-influencers-on-twitter.html

[75] https://www.tvpage.com/video-sales-are-up-by-3x/

[76] https://help.shopify.com/en/manual/reports-and-analytics/discrepancies

[77] https://www.optily.com/digital-marketing-tactics/why-its-time-to-update-your-attribution-model-in-google-analytics/

[78] https://w3techs.com/technologies/details/ta-googleanalytics

[79] https://en.wikipedia.org/wiki/Lloyd_Shapley

[80] https://towardsdatascience.com/market-mix-modeling-mmm-101-3d094df976f9

[81] https://www.thinkwithgoogle.com/marketing-strategies/data-and-measurement/marketing-mix-modeling-tutorial/

[82] https://www.facebook.com/business/news/insights/considerations-for-creating-modern-marketing-mix-models

[83] https://www.accenture.com/_acnmedia/PDF-92/Accenture-

Market-Mix-Optimization.pdf

[84] https://www.marketingweek.com/mark-ritson-brand-strategy-marketing/

[85] https://www.optily.com/ad-platforms/the-big-7-platforms-ad-revenue-2020/

Printed in Poland
by Amazon Fulfillment
Poland Sp. z o.o., Wrocław

74600470R00092